Business Guides on the Go

"Business Guides on the Go" presents cutting-edge insights from practice on particular topics within the fields of business, management, and finance. Written by practitioners and experts in a concise and accessible form the series provides professionals with a general understanding and a first practical approach to latest developments in business strategy, leadership, operations, HR management, innovation and technology management, marketing or digitalization. Students of business administration or management will also benefit from these practical guides for their future occupation/careers.

These Guides suit the needs of today's fast reader.

Cansu Hattula • Ines Köhler
Editors

Change Management Revisited

A Practitioner's Guide to Implementing Digital Solutions

 Springer

Editors
Cansu Hattula
IU International University
Hannover, Germany

Ines Köhler
Schindler (Switzerland)
Berlin, Germany

ISSN 2731-4758   ISSN 2731-4766   (electronic)
Business Guides on the Go
ISBN 978-3-031-30239-8   ISBN 978-3-031-30240-4   (eBook)
https://doi.org/10.1007/978-3-031-30240-4

This Springer imprint is published by the registered company Springer Nature Switzerland AG
The registered company address is: Gewerbestrasse 11, 6330 Cham, Switzerland

Preface

Throughout the last decade, resilience and the ability to handle change have become critical success factors for organizations. This may be why companies and practitioners have paid increasing attention to the topic of organizational change management. Although numerous change management models and theories exist and firms invest huge budgets in tools, training, and consulting projects, recent studies still show a high failure rate for change processes in the context of digital projects.

Having been part of various change projects in different organizations, we faced similar challenges while going through the process. We witnessed that the human component is key for successful change implementation. This is especially true for transformation processes related to digital products or technologies, where the focus is often on the technological changes rather than on the "soft factors".

Management or employees may be reluctant to change due to individual experiences, interests, or a lack of awareness for why the transformation needs to happen. Stakeholders may not be sufficiently informed. Important players involved in the transformation process may change and not enough time is spent to onboard the new players. People affected by the change may feel left alone with their challenges.

We would like to thank all the authors who shared their business cases and invaluable experiences. It was a pleasure working with you! Also, we appreciate the support of our families, friends, and colleagues who proof-read several chapters of this book.

The following chapters and cases show how different companies and industries incorporate the human aspect of change in their digital change projects. Overall, it is our hope that this book provides a foundation for your change projects related to digital solutions and a motivation to pay special attention to the human component in the change process. We hope that the various checklists, hands-on practice tips, and examples throughout this book will inspire you and guide you through your own change project.

Hannover, Germany   Cansu Hattula
January 2023   Ines Köhler

Contents

Change Management and Implementing Digital Solutions: An Introduction and Overview

Ines Köhler and Cansu Hattula

1 Introduction

Over the last decades, practitioners have paid increasing attention to the topic of organizational change management (Oral, 2016). Although managers invested huge amounts of budget in tools, trainings, and books, recent studies still show a high failure rate for change projects. A global survey of 3199 executives reveals that only one change project in three succeeds (McKinsey, 2009). Interestingly, the high rate of change failures has stayed constant from the seventies to the present, which shows that managers have not yet found a solution for implementing change in their organizations effectively (Oral, 2016). Additionally, more than three in five IT projects do not deliver the expected outcome for the expected costs and within the expected timeline:

I. Köhler
Schindler, Berlin, Germany

C. Hattula (✉)
IU International University of Applied Sciences, Hannover, Germany

© The Author(s), under exclusive license to Springer Nature Switzerland AG 2023
C. Hattula, I. Köhler (eds.), *Change Management Revisited*, Business Guides on the Go, https://doi.org/10.1007/978-3-031-30240-4_1

1

- 49% suffer budget overruns.
- 47% result in higher-than-expected maintenance costs.
- 41% fail to deliver the expected business value.

Since organizations tend to cover up their own failure rate, these statistics are probably understated (Simon, 2011).

But why do change efforts fail? Literature provides evidence for the main barriers to change. For instance, neglecting to form a case for urgency in the organization, failing to create a powerful coalition to enforce the change, and lacking a clear vision can stop companies from changing effectively (Kotter, 1996). If companies do not address and solve these important barriers, negative outcomes can result in practice, such as confusion, chaos, and feelings of anxiety and frustration (Oral, 2016).

Another explanation can be found in Neuroscience and the way the human brain behaves (Schwartz-Hebron, 2012).

Having been part of various change projects in different organizations, we faced similar challenges in these change processes. The human component is key for successful change implementation. For instance, many software projects in various categories and in an array of different types and sizes of organizations run into challenges because they focus on the technical work but not applying enough energy toward training, coaching, team building, and soft skills. Therefore, it is vital to address the needs and fears of all change parties in the change process to move effectively.

The following chapters and cases show how different companies and industries incorporate the human aspect in their change projects.

2   Discussion of Change Models

Change management is defined as "the process of continually renewing an organization's direction, structure and capabilities to serve the ever-changing needs of external and internal customers" (Moran & Brightman, 2001, p. 111). Further, a *change process* is about "understanding how organizational change is formulated and implemented" (Van de Ven, 1992, p. 169).

In order to implement strategic change, organizations may choose between *different implementation styles*. The choice of the style might cause or prevent conflicts that can result from different attitudes toward the change (e.g., Gupta & Govindarajan, 1984). But how can companies decide which implementation style is appropriate for their strategic change process when implementing a digital product or service? In the following, we discuss relevant theories that explain the process view on strategic change. In general, three accounts are discussed that have received particular research attention in recent years: the top-down or bottom-up approach, the planned or emergent approaches, and Staehle's (1999) three approaches to enacting change.

First, organizations might *implement a digital solution top-down or bottom-up*. A top-down approach means that the top management team develops a product strategy and communicates it downward until it reaches the frontline employees. In top-down changes, top managers generally conceive and plan the change. Middle managers, on the other hand, are responsible for the detailed coordination, implementation, and internal management of the change (Sirkin et al., 2005). In contrast, according to a bottom-up approach the strategy is developed "in the field" so that the upper levels only accept or modify it (Meffert et al., 2012, p. 780). The bottom-up approach creates conditions for direct employee participation that top-down change generally does not provide (Sirkin et al., 2005).

A second approach distinguishes between *planned and emergent change* (Bamford & Forrester, 2003). The planned approach goes hand in hand with a top-down change, whereas the emergent approach can be related to a bottom-up change. The *planned approach* emphasizes the dynamics in the change process (Burnes, 1996; Eldrod II & Tippett, 2002). It focuses on the importance of understanding the different states an organization goes through in order to move from an unsatisfactory state to a desired state (Eldrod II & Tippett, 2002). In line with this approach, Lewin (1963) determines three phases of a change process: unfreezing, moving, and freezing. First, he suggests that specific behavioral patterns in the organization need to be questioned (unfreezing). Only after the unfreezing of these patterns can the change be initiated effectively (moving). Finally, organizations should maintain the newly established patterns in the long run (freezing).

In elaborating on the planned approach to change in more detail, Fig. 1 shows *three process models of how top managers can guide change processes.* Kanter et al. (1992) present ten commandments for executing change. Kanter et al. (1992) analyze the organization and its need for change, creating a vision and a common direction, separating from the past, creating a sense of urgency, supporting a strong leadership role, lining up political sponsorship, crafting an implementation plan, developing enabling structures, communicating and reinforcing, and institutionalizing change. Second, Kotter (1996) shows eight steps for a change: establishing a sense of urgency, creating a guiding coalition, developing a vision, communicating, empowering, generating short-term wins, consolidating gains, and anchoring new approaches in the culture. Third, Luecke (2003) introduces seven steps of a change process, including mobilizing energy, developing a shared vision, identifying the leadership, focusing on results, spreading change in the organization, institutionalizing success, and monitoring. These models show several similarities. At least two of the three models include the steps of analyzing the situation, creating a vision, creating a sense of urgency, identifying leaders to sponsor the change, and communicating the change and institutionalizing it in the culture (Kanter et al., 1992; Kotter, 1996; Luecke, 2003). To conclude, these common steps are likely to be vital for guiding a change process effectively (Oral, 2016).

Although the planned approach to change is oftentimes effective, it has also *been criticized* (Burnes, 1996; Kanter et al., 1992). First, scholars have pointed out that the approach focuses on incremental change and, hence, it is not useful in situations that require quick major change (Burnes, 1996). Second, the planned approach predicts that companies can move in a pre-planned way from one stable state to another. Studies show, however, that this "freezing" phase does not match today's dynamic environment (Meffert et al., 2012, p. 776), e.g., COVID pandemic and the VUCA world. Other scholars propose that strategic change implementation is not a single linear process but rather a set of

Change Phases Lewin (1963)	Ten Commandments for Executing Change (Kanter et al., 1992)	Eight Steps for Organizational Transformation (Kotter, 1996)	Seven Steps of Change (Luecke, 2003)
I Unfreeze	1. Analyze the organization and its need for change	1. Establish a sense of urgency	1. Mobilize energy and commitment through joint identification of business problems and their solutions
II Move	2. Create a vision and a common direction	2. Create a guiding coalition	2. Develop a shared vision of how to organize and manage for competitiveness
	3. Separate from the past	3. Develop a vision and strategy	3. Identify the leadership
	4. Create a sense of urgency	4. Communicate the change	4. Focus on results, not on activities
	5. Support a strong leader role	5. Empower broad-based action	5. Start change at the periphery, then let it spread to other units without pushing it from the top
	6. Line up political sponsorship	6. Generate short-term wins	6. Institutionalize through formal policies, systems, and structures
	7. Craft an implementation plan	7. Consolidate gains and producing more change	
	8. Develop enabling structures		
	9. Communicate, involve people, and be honest		
III Freeze	10. Reinforce and institutionalize change	8. Anchor new approaches in the culture	7. Monitor and adjust strategies

Fig. 1 Models of change processes: illustration based on Todnem (2005) and Oral (2016)

simultaneous processes (Sonenshein, 2010). Third, planned change is not useful in situations where more flexibility is necessary, e.g., in a crisis situation.

In order to address the shortcomings of planned change, an *emergent approach* has become prevalent (Todnem, 2005). Rather than seeing change as a top-driven process, the emergent approach describes the change as happening from the bottom-up (Burnes, 1996). The emergent approach argues that change is quick and that it is impossible for top managers to effectively identify, plan, and implement the necessary organizational responses on their own (Kanter et al., 1992). Hence, they need to delegate the responsibility of organizational change to lower organizational levels, e.g., frontline employees or middle managers (Oral, 2016). From an emergent point of view, change should not be perceived as a series of linear actions within a given period of time, but as a continuous, open-ended process of adaptation to altering situations (Burnes, 1996). Put differently, the emergent view underlines the unpredictable nature of change (Todnem, 2005).

In addition to the above-mentioned ways, organizations increasingly use the ADKAR model to understand the human side of change. The ADKAR model focuses on individuals' change adaptation (Hiatt, 2013) and how well the individuals receive the change (see Fig. 2). The ADKAR model is sequenced by how an individual experiences the change. The ADKAR life cycle begins after identifying a change (Galli, 2018). From this initiation point, there is a framework and sequence for managing the people's side of change (Hiatt, 2013). The acronym stands for five goals that the model aims to accomplish:

1. Awareness
2. Desire
3. Knowledge
4. Ability
5. Reinforcement (Fig. 2)

Awareness happens when an organization informs employees of a need for change, for instance, the implementation of a new digital solution such as an online store (Galli, 2018). The primary issue at this stage is determining the level of change for a particular project. Desire from the employees and project team requires the motivation to participate in the change along with the ability to perform the changes. Thus, employees need knowledge of how to change and what the transformation involves. In the Ability phase, employees acquire the skills to implement change on a day-to-day basis. Lastly, reinforcement is needed to maintain and sustain change in the project (Galli, 2018; Hiatt, 2013).

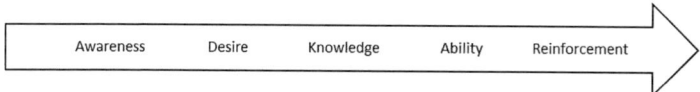

Fig. 2 ADKAR model [based on Hiatt (2013)]

A typical reason why change projects can fail is that the process starts directly with step 3—the knowledge, and the creation of awareness and desire is not highlighted enough. If change agents are not aware of and desire a certain change, it is unlikely that they will support it.

3   Transformation Processes When Implementing Digital Solutions

This book focuses on transformation processes linked to the implementation of digital products or solutions. This includes third-party solutions as well as own developments of an organization. While the introduction or substitution of a software platform is often seen primarily as a technology change, the management of the transformation plays a significant role when it comes to achieving the expected benefit (Simon, 2011).

Throughout this book, the following transformation processes are described and discussed:

Part I: Transformation Processes Related to Digital Products

(a) Introduction of a new digital product that is the main business model
The classical example for this type of transformation would be an app or online solution that is the main business driver or main offering of an organization. One example for this is the app "Taxfix" as a new way to make payments or hand in tax declarations (O'Hear, 2018).

In this case, change management is needed to introduce a new customer journey or manage new customer expectations as well as the transformation the company undergoes while launching the new business model. An example of this type of change can be found in the paper written by Würtenberger.

(b) Introduction of a new digital product complementing the existing business model

This sort of transformation happens when an organization introduces a new customer-facing application that complements the existing offering or adds new self-services to it. All kinds of customer portals can be examples of this type, a common one would be popular grocery shopping apps like "Bringmeister" or "Rewe." They complement the existing offering, but come with some changes to the customer journey, changes in the way services are performed, and the need to complement the digital product with other touchpoints (e.g., a new form of customer service).

The digitization of sales processes may change the way organizations have worked for decades and can significantly affect the task profile of job roles. Not taking care of managing these changes, including internal mindset and culture may lead to undesired results, such as employee resistance to change (Shina et al., 2022).

This type of change is discussed in the papers written by Nenstiel-Köhling/Exler and D'Aniello.

(c) Introduction of a new technology or platform

The introduction of a new technology or platform can range from the introduction of new apps and easy-to-use SaaS systems to the introduction of more complex platforms affecting tens of thousands of users. For larger projects, software vendors and implementation partners get involved. This may lead to additional complexity, more challenging communication processes, and a lack of accountability in the organization that is going through the change.

Transformations related to system implementations can have different challenges. If an existing "legacy" system is replaced it may be a challenge to transition to a "new way of doing things." "Greenfield" implementations, on the other hand, come with an increased need for training and knowledge built up, but with users happy to have any system (instead of nothing) and therefore more likely to embrace the change (Simon, 2011, p. 71).

This type of transformation is discussed in the papers written by D'Aniello and Schoder et al.

Part II: Cultural and Organizational Transformation Processes
Another type of transformation that includes a more structural and cultural component is currently going on in digital organizations. The traditional role of IT in companies is evolving and they need to form a new identity to embrace current changes regarding technologies, user needs, and environments (Stockhall, 2019).

These dynamics also impact organizations that develop and market digital products and solutions, especially when they are in exploratory stages (early-stage startups). The importance of the environment in which the change is taking place and the relevance of managing resistance is an important success factors for transformation processes (Kotter, 1996). In most cases change management approaches have to be adapted and tailored to the specific organizational setting (Prosci, 2020).

Transformation processes around culture and organizational setup are discussed in the papers written by Henriot Arsever and Würtenberger.

One point to consider is also the setup of external and internal players during the transformation processes. Oftentimes, for the implementation of new technologies an external software vendor and an external implementation partner add complexity to the stakeholder map. The perspective of the implementation partner is discussed in the paper by D'Aniello.

4   Enablers of Transformation in Digital Contexts

Human-Centered and User-Centered Designs
The orchestration of people involved in software projects is a key success factor. "There are many factors that may lead to project failure; most of them being of nontechnical nature, (...). By looking at these factors in more detail, it becomes obvious that it is all about people, either as providers of input, as members of a project team or stakeholders of a project or as users of the project result" (Maedche et al., 2012, p. 2).

In addition to the people involved in the management of a digital project also user expectations have changed significantly throughout the last years. A smooth, easy-to-understand, and intuitive user experience is no longer a nice-to-have for any kind of digital solution, it is a must-have and has become essential for adoption and economic success. This is valid both in a B2B and in a B2C context (Maedche et al., 2012).

Organizations that embrace a human-centered perspective when it comes to the management of digital initiatives tend to have a stronger focus on the proactive management of transformations. A user-centered development approach in software development usually also comes with a more agile, iterative development process that is much more open to embracing change than a traditional waterfall approach (March, 2018).

Agile Methodologies

The use of agile methodologies (in contrast to traditional waterfall methodologies) is in fact another enabler for change. While waterfall projects are organized in a linear way that requires each project phase to be closed before the team can start to work on the next phase, agile methodologies allow for contemporary work on different phases at the same time, resulting in more flexibility and more frequent interaction with stakeholders (Hooray, 2022).

Technologies, user requirements, and external factors may change during a project. This is true especially for initiatives that are stretched across longer time periods. Agile methodologies were developed to incorporate these changes and allow for a quicker delivery time even if requirements or circumstances change at a late stage in the project. Stakeholder feedback—including user feedback—is gathered frequently to ensure user expectations are met and a user-centric approach is applied (Hooray, 2022). Another benefit of agile methodologies is the empowerment of the team. While waterfall projects are often managed according to a traditional top-down approach, agile management gives a much stronger position to the whole team involved, leading to higher motivation and accountability (Hooray, 2022).

Summing up, agile methodologies drive accountability, flexibility, and an open-minded attitude and can be a strong enabler of transformation.

New Work

New work and especially more remote setups have led to teams spread out across different time zones and represent new challenges to transformation processes. Communication processes and documentation of work need to be organized in new ways and new mechanisms for feedback processes need to be found. While new work enables and promotes digital collaboration at large it is not necessarily an enabler of the transformation processes. But it is hugely important to take into account the specific needs of teams and organizations working across locations and time zones when it comes to the orchestration of change management activities (Baker, 2021).

Inclusion and Diversity

Inclusive working cultures and diverse teams are an important enabler for change processes that should never be overlooked.

There are by now countless studies highlighting the advantage of diversity in teams. One of them is a McKinsey report titled "Why Diversity Matters" (Hunt et al., 2015). It confirms that employing a diverse range of people leads to better financial results. This is linked back to diverse teams being better at creative solution thinking. However, the diversity of team members needs to be complemented by an inclusive setup, making sure all team members feel comfortable and empowered to express opinions and points of view (Hunt et al., 2015). The innovative and agile mindset resulting from diverse and inclusive teams show to be especially valuable during transitions, when new perspectives and an open mind are needed to handle the human nature of resisting changes.

Another thing to be kept in mind by change managers when it comes to diversity is the fact that different personalities may handle change in a different way. There are diverse backgrounds, diverse experiences, and diverse fears associated with change leading to different emotional barriers. A "one-size-fits-all" approach will not work to overcome them all—and this is valid both for the individual and the organizational levels.

Organizational Culture

Another key enabler for transformation processes is organizational culture. The famous quote "culture eats strategy for breakfast" by management consultant Peter F. Ducker states that a strategy will never be successful unless the organizational culture is fit to meet the strategy.

For successful transformation processes, this implies that a change outcome can only be successful if the organizational culture represents an environment ready to welcome that change. Bryson (2008) confirms the important link between organizational change and organizational culture as a critical variable in change processes.

Based on the openness to change of an organization, the challenges in a transformation process may vary. An organization very open to change needs mostly governance and steering (in ADKAR language this would mean that the awareness and desire are already met). A more change-resistant culture needs activation (aka awareness and desire), otherwise, it will not be willing to engage in the change process to begin with.

5 Brief Outlook on Cases and Topics Discussed in the Papers

In the *first part* of this book, we focus on transformation processes related to digital products.

The challenge of implementing new technology in expert-driven organizations is discussed in the chapter "Managing Digital-Driven Change in Expert Organizations: The Case of a Swiss Hospital." *Schoder, Pieper,* and *Widmer* describe the experience of a medium size Swiss hospital during the launch of a new hospital information system. The paper puts a specific focus on the healthcare industry, but their learnings can be transferred to any kind of organization that is highly dependent on a group of experts. The authors explain how to make sure that the team members are aware of the need for change and subsequently embrace and support the change process. The case also gives interesting insights into the digitization challenges of the Swiss healthcare industry.

The usage of agile methodologies in digital transformation projects is the main topic of the paper written by *D'Aniello*. In the chapter "Applying Agile Methodologies in Digital Transformation Processes: Learnings and Challenges from 10 years of Consulting Experience," she reflects on her experiences, gathered in a decade of consulting as Senior Manager at Deloitte Digital and assesses how the methodologies were adapted to individual organizational settings. Her article presents three different cases, all related to the introduction of software or new digital products. For each case, the pros and cons as well as the lessons learned are shared. The paper comes with a lot of valuable hacks and actionable insights for the setup of transformation projects.

In the chapter "From Input to Outcomes: Bayer's Digital Transformation of Agricultural Business Exploration," *Nenstiel-Köhling* and *Exler* describe the change process related to the evolution of Bayer's agricultural portfolio by enhancing it via digital solutions. They investigate the redefinition of the relevant market and value pool and address the disruption of the market by a major competitive threat coming from non-traditional competitors.

In Part II, we look at cultural and organizational transformation processes related to digital organizations and environments.

Henriot Arsever shares her experience in transforming an IT organization at a large logistics company. She realized quickly that the challenges of her team went beyond technological topics. Inspired by the Sociocracy 3.0 Framework, she initiated a major initiative with the objective to change the way of working, the delivery model, and the image of the organization. The paper is full of interesting insights, learnings along the way and very concrete, actionable tools that can support this kind of transformation process. It also gives a comprehensive understanding of the identity challenge many traditional IT organizations are currently facing.

A cultural transformation in a very different organizational setting is the focus of the chapter "Pivoting to a Web3 Product and Building a Healthy Remote Culture with Human-Centric Leadership." *Würtenberger*, CHRO at Flooz, an early-stage startup that operates with a fully remote organization, describes how she built up a heart-centered company culture during a significant strategy reorientation of the company.

Communication tools and approaches are described that can help to scale and transform company culture in fully remote organizations.

The importance of community building and reflection is the central theme of chapter "Community Building in Change Processes". In this paper, *Ramos*, Community Host, Facilitator, and Learning Designer, look at the individual layer of transformation and presents how she built up an easily replicable process for the reflection of change processes.

The tool described was initiated by her during the second COVID-19 wave in Portugal and participants have transferred the process into their organizations. Lessons learnt and lots of actionable how-to-knowledge are shared for anyone who wants to use the power of community and reflection to support a change process.

References

Baker, M. (2021). *4 modes of collaboration are key to success in hybrid work*. Gartner.

Bamford, D. R., & Forrester, P. L. (2003). Managing planned and emergent change within an operations management environment. *International Journal of Operations & Production Management, 23*(5), 546–564.

Bryson, J. (2008). Dominant, emergent, and residual culture: The dynamics of organizational change. *Journal of Organizational Change Management, 21*(6), 743–757.

Burnes, B. (1996). No such thing as a "one best way" to manage organizational change. *Management Decision, 34*(10), 11–18.

Eldrod, P. D., II, & Tippett, D. D. (2002). The "death valley" of change. *Journal of Organizational Change Management, 15*(3), 273–291.

Galli, B. J. (2018). Change management models: A comparative analysis and concerns. *IEEE Engineering Management Review, 46*(3), 124–132.

Gupta, A. K., & Govindarajan, V. (1984). Business unit strategy, managerial characteristics, and business unit effectiveness at strategy implementation. *Academy of Management Journal, 27*(1), 25–41.

Hiatt, J. M. (2013). *Employees survival guide to change: The complete guide to surviving and thriving during organizational change*. Prosci Research.

Hooray, L. (2022). *Agile vs. waterfall: Which project management methodology is best for you?* Retrieved via Forbes Advisor, January 6, from https://www.forbes.com/advisor/business/agile-vs-waterfall-methodology/

Hunt, V., Layton, D., & Prince, S. (2015). *Why diversity matters*. Retrieved via McKinsey & Company, January 7, from https://www.mckinsey.com/capabilities/people-and-organizational-performance/our-insights/why-diversity-matters

Kanter, R. M., Stein, B. A., & Jick, T. D. (1992). *The challenge of organizational change*. The Free Press.

Kotter, J. P. (1996). *Leading change*. Harvard Business Press.

Lewin, K. (1963). *Feldtheorie in den Sozialwissenschaften*. Bern.

Luecke, R. (2003). *Managing change and transition*. Harvard Business Press.

Maedche, A., Botzenhardt, A., & Neer, L. (2012). *Software for people. Fundamentals, Trends and practices*. Springer Nature.

March, S. (2018). *A practical guide to designing better products and services*. Kogan Page.

McKinsey. (2009). *The irrational side of change management*. Retrieved from http://www.mckinsey.com/insights/organization/the_irrational_side_of_change_management [accessed on 04.12.2022]

Meffert, H., Burmann, C., & Kirchgeorg, M. (2012). *Marketing: Grundlagen marktorientierter Unternehmensführung; Konzepte – Instrumente – Praxisbeispiele* (11th ed.). Gabler.

Moran, J. W., & Brightman, B. K. (2001). Leading organizational change. *Career Development International, 6*(2), 111–118.

O'Hear, S. (2018). *Berlin's Taxfix, a mobile assistant for filing your taxes, picks up $13M led by Valar Ventures*. Retrieved via Techcrunch, January 22, 2023, from https://techcrunch.com/2018/08/09/taxfix/

Oral, C. (2016). *Middle managers as change agents—An investigation of their role in a top-driven change process towards end-customer orientation, dissertation*. University of St. Gallen.

Prosci. (2020). *Best practices in change management executive summary* (11th ed.). Prosci Research. Retrieved January 6, from https://www.prosci.com/resources/articles/change-management-best-practices

Schwartz-Hebron, R. (2012). Using neuroscience to effect change in the workplace. *Employment Relations Today, 39*(2), 11–15.

Shina, P., Sahay, D., Shastri, A., & Lorimer, S. E. (2022). How to digitalize your sales organization. *Harvard Business Review*.

Simon, P. (2011). *Why new systems fail, revised edition: An insider's guide to successful IT projects*. Course Technology.

Sirkin, H. L., Keenan, P., & Jackson, A. (2005). *Top down organizational change initiatives*. Retrieved via HBR, January 6, 2023, from https://hbr.org/2005/10/the-hard-side-of-change-management

Sonenshein, S. (2010). We're changing—Or are we? untangling the role of progressive, regressive, and stability narratives during strategic change implementation. *Academy of Management Journal, 53*(3), 477–512.

Staehle, W. H. (1999). *Management: Eine verhaltenswissenschaftliche Perspektive* (8th ed.). Gabler.

Stockhall, J. (2019). *The changing role of IT.* Retrieved via Forbes, January 22, from   https://www.forbes.com/sites/forbestechcouncil/2019/08/02/the-changing-role-of-it/

Todnem, B. R. (2005). Organizational change management: A critical review. *Journal of Change Management, 5*(4), 369–380.

Van de Ven, A. H. (1992). Suggestions for studying strategy process: A research note. *Strategic Management Journal, 13*(5), 169–188.

Ines Köhler is a martech and digital strategy expert with 15 years of industry experience in corporates and startups. She has completed her studies in communication science and business administration at Freie Universität of Berlin and LUISS Guido Carli in Rome. Her current role focuses on digital strategy and transformation at Schindler Group. Her previous role at Canto, a leading provider of digital asset management solutions, helped her to get deep insights into the operations of software development and go-to-market strategies for digital products. At Hasso-Plattner Institute, she took care of communicating research results and use cases of cutting-edge technologies. Ines is passionate about new work, change management, yoga, and personal development.

Cansu Hattula is a professor at IU International University of Applied Sciences and teaches consumer behavior and international marketing to bachelor, master, and MBA students. She has completed her studies in business administration at the University of Hannover and her PhD at the University of St. Gallen. Her research interests include change management and marketing strategy. In her PhD, she analyzes how middle management can implement marketing change in their organizations. She gained international working experience in Germany, Switzerland, and the UK with various corporations and startups such as Deutsche Messe AG, Too Good To Go, and Bayer CropScience. Cansu is passionate about the human side of change management and how to implement new marketing strategies and technologies in organizations.

Part I

Transformation Processes Related to Digital Products

Managing Digital-Driven Change in Expert Organizations: The Case of a Swiss Hospital

Johannes Schoder, Jan Pieper, and Philippe K. Widmer

1 Introduction

Healthcare is a typical example of a service sector that comprises various kinds of expert organizations,[1] especially hospitals. In hospitals, many different expert groups need to collaborate, and each of them tends to strongly identify with their respective profession. A key challenge to developing shared goals and mutual understanding across these

---

[1] Companies in which the employed experts become the actual product or service will subsequently be referred to as expert organizations. Typical expert organizations are universities, law and consulting firms, or medical organizations such as hospitals or medical group practices (Rybnicek et al., 2016).

J. Schoder (✉)
Baden-Wuerttemberg Cooperative State University, Loerrach, Germany
e-mail: schoder@dhbw-loerrach.de

J. Pieper
IU International University, Erfurt, Germany
e-mail: jan.pieper@iu.org

P. K. Widmer
Spital Limmatal, Zurich, Switzerland

© The Author(s), under exclusive license to Springer Nature Switzerland AG 2023
C. Hattula, I. Köhler (eds.), *Change Management Revisited*, Business Guides on the Go, https://doi.org/10.1007/978-3-031-30240-4_2

heterogeneous groups is to overcome systematic differences in professional language, work practices, problem-solving approaches, and subcultures.

According to Drucker (2007) and Mintzberg (1980) leading such expert organizations is one of the biggest organizational challenges because of the critical role of their members. Thus, expert organizations tend to be particularly resistant to any aspect of change (Pepper, 2002).

Digitalization is considered one of the major disruptors in the medical field. It offers significant efficiency gains in the provision of healthcare, e.g., it improves the coordination of care along the patient journey and facilitates the collaboration between healthcare providers resulting in overall cost reductions (McKinsey, 2021; Ancker, 2015; Aue et al., 2016; Rahimi, 2019). However, the switch from paper-based to digital solutions implies standardization of processes which requires organizational change. Given the rigidity and heterogeneity of expert organizations, managing this change seems to be particularly challenging. Accordingly, Berg (2001) reports more failure than success stories when it comes to the successful implementation of new information technology (IT) systems inside healthcare organizations, especially hospitals.

This chapter aims to provide insight into successfully managing digital-driven change by analyzing the case of a Swiss medium-sized hospital's implementation of a new IT system. We start with a brief summary of the current knowledge about the phenomenon of resistance to change in healthcare. Next, we take a closer look at the Swiss hospital market concerning its digital infrastructure. We then critically evaluate the practical use of Kotter's (1995, 1996) classic change management model, which served as a conceptual foundation to guide the hospital's change initiative. Next, we provide recommendations for minor, yet specific adaptations when applying the model in expert organizations.

Our insights are not only relevant for hospital managers dealing with digitally driven change, but for all managers of expert organizations looking for a compelling change management concept. Furthermore, our case allows us to shed light on the competitive relevance of learning curve effects in digital change management projects, especially for smaller players who cannot match their bigger competitors' digital scalability and bargaining power over external service providers.

2   The Phenomenon of Resistance to Change in Healthcare Organizations

The literature offers two possible and related explanations of why the digital-driven change in healthcare organizations may be opposed.

The first, market-based explanation, highlights the rather hostile environment in healthcare with respect to process innovations. IT-based innovations are mostly process innovations.[2] Process innovations produce existing products at lower costs. In the context of healthcare, this means that IT systems contribute to more efficient delivery of existing healthcare services. However, in the presence of social insurance where utilization of healthcare services is free of charge, consumers rarely have a higher willingness to pay for process innovations (Zweifel, 2021). They rather value new medical treatments. Consequently, healthcare providers have limited incentives to adopt process innovations since hardly any new patients can be attracted (Zweifel, 2022; Brauns, 2015). This may explain why the digital maturity level of healthcare organizations is lower than that of organizations of other industries and points toward a large potential for efficiency gains (McKinsey, 2021).

The second (individual-based) explanation refers to the members of the healthcare organization and their particular interests. As the medical staff is one of the primary resources for producing healthcare within a hospital, they play a crucial role. Particularly physicians who have taken the Hippocratic oath, possess a significant level of autonomy when it comes to treatment decisions and the level of effort they put in. According to Stoddard et al. (2001), professional autonomy (along with relative income) is indeed one of the most important determinants of physicians' career satisfaction in the USA. When it comes to digitally driven change

---

[2] Economists distinguish between three types of innovations organizational, process, and product innovations (Damanpour, 1991). While product innovations bestow new attributes on goods, process, and organizational innovations leave attributes unchanged.

they are often skeptically fearing a loss of this autonomy (see Lamothe & Dufour, 2007; Pepper, 2002), especially if it implies standardization of care which may force them to perform their functions faster (Nash, 1998). However, in this context Cocchi (2014) reports that physicians instead fear a drop in their productivity, over-reliance on electronic health records (EHR) systems, and interference with patient communication. Alexander and Ballou (2018) show evidence of increased burnout because physicians are clicking pull-down menus and typing rather than interacting with patients. According to Drummond et al. (2009), poorly designed and implemented IT systems may add to the high cognitive burden of physicians, including distraction and physical absence from the patient. Barrett (2017) finds resistance against EHRs not only by physicians but also nurses and hospital employees. Especially the seniority positively affects the level of resistance in his statistical analysis. Lapointe and Rivard (2006) and Bhattacherjee and Himet (2007) attributed the failure of new IT system implementations in several US hospitals due to an insufficient integration of the medical staff.

In Conclusion, the healthcare sector remains a challenging area for implementing new IT systems, mainly because of the limited incentives for cost-saving process innovations and the members' resistance to change. Therefore, any digital-driven change initiative needs to pay special attention to the human aspect of change, viz. integrating and embracing its members in a "smart" way.

The Swiss Hospital Market and the Digital Infrastructure

The Swiss healthcare system is characterized by its decentralized federal structure and its excellent access to care (Zweifel, 2000). With cantons being responsible for hospital capacity planning and financing, 99.8% of the population can reach a hospital within a 30-min drive (Estevez & Cosandey, 2022). Due to the ever-increasing healthcare costs, several healthcare reforms have been put into place to increase competition between hospitals (Cosandey et al., 2018; Widmer, 2014). Accordingly, since 2012 the number of hospitals has decreased from almost 300 to currently 276 (FSO, 2021). The trend of consolidation is expected to persist in the future, increasing the demand for efficient delivery of healthcare services.

Whereas in the past, the emphasis was mainly on renovating hospital facilities (Medinside, 2016; PWC, 2013), the focus now has shifted to updating the hospital's digital infrastructure in the hope of gaining a competitive advantage. According to McKinsey (2021), Swiss hospitals have begun increasing their investment in IT, but there is still significant untapped potential for growth in this area. Overall, Switzerland's digital infrastructure is still falling behind that of pioneering countries like Denmark and Estonia (Thiel et al., 2018; Synpulse, 2020). In this context, the interoperability of IT systems remains an unresolved challenge that would be essential to improve the coordination of care across hospitals and other healthcare providers. This challenge arises from Switzerland's federal structure, which makes it more challenging to implement standardized systems than in more centralized countries like France or Germany (Golder et al., 2021).

One of the largest IT investments and major lever to increase efficiency is the hospital information system (HIS), which integrates all aspects of a hospital operation, such as medical, administrative, and financial. A well-functioning HIS is an important tool to improve the planning and the organization of patient treatment, clinical documentation, and overall hospital capacity planning (Fleßa, 2018). Although more than 90% of Swiss hospitals have implemented a Health Information System (HIS), many remain dissatisfied with the application's inability to meet their basic requirements, including stable performance, adaptation to existing processes, and interoperability with other systems (Angerer et al., 2021). Correspondingly, more than a dozen hospitals are currently changing their provider or updating their HIS (Toedtli, 2020).

To sum up, the competitive Swiss hospital market points toward a rather favorable environment with respect to process innovations. Hence, resistance to change should rather be observed at the individual and not at the organizational level. Next, given that many hospitals are unsatisfied with their current IT systems, adapting a standardized IT system according to the specific needs and existing processes of a hospital seems to be an important success factor. However, this is especially challenging for smaller hospitals which neither have the necessary bargaining power while negotiating customized solutions with IT providers nor do they have the same advantages from economies of scale such as hospital chains when implementing new IT systems.

3 Kotter's Classic Change Management Model

Considering the empirical evidence that between one-third and 80% of organizational change initiatives fail (e.g., Beer & Nohria, 2000; Higgs & Rowland, 2000; Hirschhorn, 2002; Sirkin et al., 2005; Kotter, 2008; Meaney & Pung, 2008; Whelan-Berry & Somerville, 2010), the need for conceptual guidance to support managers in the field of change management is obvious.

A classic change management model, proposed by John P. Kotter, was first published in a 1995 Harvard Business Review article. In 1996, the same model was published in greater detail in his book *Leading Change*. This book became a business bestseller and remains a key reference in the field of change management with over 18,000 citations in Google Scholar. One interesting aspect of Kotter's (1996) book is that there are neither footnotes nor references. Although no bibliography can be found, his work has had tremendous practical and academic success.

According to Kotter, the eight steps to transforming an organization are as follows:

Step 1: Establish a Sense of Urgency
According to Kotter (1995), successful change efforts must begin with evaluating the focal company's competitive situation, technological trends, and financial performance. Bold or risky actions are generally required for creating a strong sense of urgency (Kotter, 1995). He argues that this essential first step requires close cooperation at the leadership level who must deeply understand the need for change. Otherwise, the change agents will not have enough power and credibility to initiate the required change program. Kotter (1996) also recommends the use of consultants as a tactic for creating a sense of urgency and challenging the status quo.

Step 2: Create A Guiding Coalition

Kotter (1996) claims that no one person can single-handedly lead and manage the change process in an organization. Putting together the right "guiding coalition" of people to lead a change initiative is critical to its success. This guiding coalition should be made up of people with the following four characteristics (Kotter, 1996, p. 53):

- Position power: Enough key players on board so that those left out cannot block progress.
- Expertise: All relevant points of view should be represented so that informed intelligent decisions can be made.
- Credibility: The group should be seen and respected by those in the firm so that the group's pronouncements will be taken seriously by other employees.
- Leadership: The group should have enough proven leaders to be able to drive the change process.

Step 3: Develop a Vision and Strategy

The first task of the guiding coalition from Kotter's Step 2 is to formulate a "clear and sensible vision" for the transformation effort (Kotter, 1996, p. 70). Without such a vision, change efforts can become confusing, incompatible, and ineffective (Kotter, 1996).

Step 4: Communicate the Change Vision

Communication is a critical element of the organizational change process as it can reduce uncertainty (Bordia et al., 2004). Kotter suggests ensuring that the change vision is repeatable as "ideas sink in deeply only after they have been heard many times" (Kotter, 1996, p. 90). He also maintains that "two-way communication is always more powerful than one-way communication" (Kotter, 1996, p. 90).

Step 5: Empower Broad-Based Action

Compelling communication of the vision across the organization can encourage employees to try new ideas (Kotter, 1995). However, communication alone is insufficient. Employees also need support to overcome obstacles to the change vision (Kotter, 1995). Typically, empowering employees involves addressing four major obstacles: structures, skills, systems, and supervisors (Kotter, 1996, p. 102).

Step 6: Generate Short-Term Wins

In Kotter's (1995) view, seeing real changes happening as well as working and recognizing the work being done toward the long-term vision is critical. Short-term wins illustrate that change efforts are paying off (Kotter, 1996). Such wins help the guiding coalition test the vision against real conditions, convince critics, and make adjustments if necessary (Kotter, 1996). Short-term wins also provide opportunities to celebrate and reward those working for change (Kotter, 1996).

Step 7: Consolidate Gains and Produce More Change

Kotter (1995) warns that it may be tempting for managers to declare victory after the first signs of performance improvement are visible. As new processes can regress, however, leaders should use short-term wins to tackle other issues, such as systems and structures that hinder the change initiative. While leaders generally need to prove the new way is working, first successes can also serve to neutralize cynics and self-centered opponents (Kotter, 1996).

Step 8: Anchor New Approaches in the Corporate Culture

Kotter (1995) believes that new behaviors are subject to degradation if they are not rooted in social norms and shared values once the pressure for change drops. He regards two factors as critical to institutionalize change in corporate culture:

1. Showing employees "how the new approaches, behaviors and attitudes have helped improve performance" (Kotter, 1996, p. 67).
2. Ensuring that "the next generation of management personifies the new approach" (Kotter, 1996, p. 67).

Kotter recommends following these eight steps in sequence and avoiding extended overlapping of the steps. While this claim lacks empirical validation (Appelbaum et al., 2012), Kotter's eight steps remain an excellent starting point for managers implementing change in their organizations. In practice, it may be useful to account for contextual variables and adapt the model accordingly (Graetz & Smith, 2010; Dopson et al., 2008).

4   Implementation Process in the Medium-Sized Hospital

Only recently, the focal hospital moved into a new building. In contrast to the new physical infrastructure the digital infrastructure was outdated. The historically grown HIS suffered from complexity and instability. Hence, it neither contributed to efficient planning and organization of patient treatment nor was it ready for future requirements such as the exchange of patient data across other healthcare providers. Considering the competitive environment in which Swiss hospitals operate, updating the HIS seemed to be essential for the head of corporate development. However, not only is an update of HIS considered necessary but basically the whole IT architecture and application landscape needed to be updated. Building on the knowledge from previous IT projects, the head of corporate development designed a unique approach that was tailored to the specific situation of the medium-sized hospital and accounted for the challenges described in Sect. 2. In the following, we describe the different implementation phases of the digital initiative and compare them with Kotter's classic change model (1996).

(a) *Establishing legitimation of the digital initiative at C-level*

The legitimation has been established through three different steps. First, the problems of end-users of the current IT systems have been made transparent. Second, the underlying root causes have been identified. Third, the consequences of what would happen if the status quo would remain have been demonstrated (in the worst-case scenario it would endanger the survival of the hospital). This proceeding is in line with Kotter (1996), who put the creation of a sense of urgency on top of his change steps.

(b) *Defining the target picture*

The following questions helped to derive the target picture: How can the root causes be solved and what measures are needed for the solution?

At the beginning of the digital initiative, there was a wide disagreement about the target picture. Therefore, the head of corporate development needed to provide clear answers to the questions mentioned above.

Next, the target picture has been subdivided into different stages in order to make them easier to navigate and to improve comprehensiveness. Based on the target picture, guiding principles have been defined.

This proceeding is pretty much in line with Kotter's third step (*develop a vision and strategy*). However, it puts less emphasis on the development of a vision for change, which seems to be central for Kotter.

(c) *Communicating the content of the digital initiative.*

To receive support from the board of directors it was essential to describe and communicate the content of the digital initiative in an understandable non-technical language. Here, one of the key challenges was how to maintain a consistent and coordinated communication of the change initiative (see below, phase d project organization). In contrast to Kotter's fourth step (*communicate vision*) which emphasizes the repetition of the vision, a compelling, short, and easy-to-understand storyline seems to be the key to success in our case.

(d) *Organization and importance of the user group in the digital initiative*

The digital initiative has been linked and aligned with the overall hospital strategy. This contributed to a further legitimation of the initiative. The organization of the project has been separated from the existing organizational structure. In this way, the relevance and priority of the digital initiative could be further highlighted. However, in order to maintain strong ties to the existing organization a so-called user group has been established. It consisted of managers of each clinical division, who were ranked at the second highest hierarchy level of the organization (CEO-1 level). One of the key challenges was to select the "right" managers for this task. Since they needed to be, on the one hand, well respected in their clinical division, but bold enough to limit their interests in order to advance the entire organization.

This user group is of particular relevance for several reasons. First, it should limit the sometimes-limitless desires of the different clinical divisions. Second, it ensures a consistent compliance and communication of the already defined guiding principles. Third, thanks to its close link to the operational processes the user group can scale its efforts in the implementation phase by involving their respective team members. Fourth, the user group has been provided with financial authority at a very early stage of the digital initiative. This was needed in order to speed up decision-making processes and to enable quick wins. Thus, the user group becomes an important element for driving the organizational transformation that the digital initiative implied (the digital initiative was not just another IT project). In this way, the head of corporate development integrated the organization at an early stage without paralyzing the project through too many stakeholders.

Phase d is in line with Kotter's second (*create a guiding coalition*), fifth (*empower broad-based action*), and sixth step (*generate short-term wins*) but are adapted to the specific circumstances of an expert organization.

To sum up, the steps undertaken were mostly in line with the framework of Kotter.

However, two deviations from Kotter's change model stand out. First, Kotter's third step (*develop a vision and strategy*) has been adopted. Instead of formulating a vision, efforts have been directed toward the formulation of tangible objectives which have been projected on a realistic roadmap. Acknowledging the complexity of a hospital and also the fact that healthcare in a hospital is not changing revolutionarily in the next few years, this down-to-earth approach seems to be sensible. It also has the advantage that the involved members of the hospital can associate something very concrete with the digital initiative (given its goals and roadmap), and that unrealistic desires could be avoided. However, the specificity of the initiative comes at a loss of flexibility. Second, the transfer of financial authority to the user group is somehow left out in Kotter's change model. Since IT projects usually require large amounts of financial resources, Kotter's framework should be adapted accordingly. However, this is not a finding specific to expert organizations.

The success of the digital initiative cannot be evaluated yet because it is still in progress.[3] Based on the experience to date, however, two key challenges can already be identified:

- The user group and its members play a crucial role in this digital initiative. Thus, a specific onboarding process can be helpful to develop a shared understanding of the project so that all project team members approach their tasks with a "can do" mindset.
- While the success of the digital initiative is important, the continuity of the hospital's day-to-day operations must clearly be prioritized. Thus, clear project planning and close coordination with operations are crucial to avoid potential conflicts over scarce resources.

5   Conclusion

The healthcare sector remains a challenging area for implementing new IT systems due to the rather limited incentives for cost-saving process innovations and to its rather change-resistant members. In comparison to most other countries, including Germany, intensive competition in the Swiss hospital market provides strong incentives to develop and exploit process innovations. In this context, the critical factor tends to be rather the hospitals' change-resistant expert members. In countries with less competitive hospital markets, the critical factor may rather be the lack of incentives to innovate in the first place.

The eight steps of Kotter's classical change management offer a good starting point for digital-driven change initiatives in expert organizations such as hospitals. However, the change management model needs to account for the critical role of its members. In this guise, the Swiss hospital offers an innovative approach, how to integrate its members, and to

---

[3] This is also why step seven and eight of Kotter's change model is not yet addressed.

avoid resistance to change. Especially the project organization together with the creation and composition of the user group is of ample relevance. Integrating its members without paralyzing the change process seems to be the key to successful change management, as in the spirit of a conventional wisdom "too many cooks spoil the broth."

Finally, the setup of the whole digital initiative would not have been possible without the lessons learned from previous IT projects, including and particularly failed ones. The more general learning seems to be that smaller hospitals—or expert organizations in general—should try to compensate for their competitive disadvantage (in terms of limited negotiation power and lack of economies of scale) by establishing a culture of failure tolerance and effective learning from the organization's own experience. To effectively learn from its own experience, the focal hospital of our study did not use any formal knowledge management approach, but the organization hugely benefited from a high degree of continuity in the relevant leadership positions.

We offer the following lessons learnt which may be of interest to managers of other expert organizations such as universities or law firms:

1. Formulate realistic objectives instead of intangible visions to enhance understanding among all experts.
2. Put the project organization outside the conventional organization hierarchy to avoid paralysis.
3. Form a small but well-respected user group with a close link to the operational divisions to scale change efforts and provide them with financial authority to speed up decision-making and facilitate quick wins.
4. Delegate responsibility. Project team members from all different organizational divisions who receive responsibility tend to be more committed. A critical requirement, however, is a shared understanding among all members of the project's goals. Members may need to be continuously encouraged to think of the project's contribution to the organization as a whole—and not to their division only.

References

Alexander, A., & Ballou, K. (2018). Work-life balance, burnout, and the electronic health record. *The American Journal of Medicine, 131*(8), 857–858.

Ancker, J. (2015). Associations between healthcare quality and use of electronic health record functions in ambulatory care. *Journal of the American Medical Informatics Association, 22*, 864–871.

Angerer, A., Hollenstein, E., & Russ, C. (2021). *Der Digitale Health Report 21/22: Die Zukunft des Schweizer Gesundheitswesens.* Retrieved September 1, 2022, from https://www.zhaw.ch/storage/hochschule/medien/news/2021/210914-digital-health-report-2021.pdf

Appelbaum, S., Habashy, S., Malo, J., & Shafiq, H. (2012). Back to the future: Revisiting Kotter's 1996 change model. *Journal of Management Development, 31*(8), 764–782.

Aue, G., Biesdorf, S., & Henke, N. (2016). e-health 2.0: How health systems can gain a leadership role in digital health. *Research Action, 1*, 1–5.

Barrett, A. (2017). Electronic Health Record (EHR) Organizational change: Explaining resistance through profession, organizational experience, and EHR communication quality. *Health Communication, 33*(4), 1–11.

Beer, M., & Nohria, N. (2000). *Breaking the code of change.* Harvard Business School Press.

Berg, M. (2001). Implementing information systems in health care organizations: Myths and challenges. *International Journal of Medical Information, 64*, 143–156.

Bhattacherjee, A., & Himet, N. (2007). Physicians' resistance toward healthcare information technology: A theoretical model and empirical test. *European Journal of Information Systems, 16*, 725–737.

Bordia, P., Hunt, E., Paulsen, N., Tourish, D., & DiFonzo, N. (2004). Uncertainty during organizational change: Is it all about control? *European Journal of Work and Organizational Psychology, 13*, 345–365.

Brauns, H.-J. (2015). *Presidential address to DGTelmed's tenth anniversary.* Retrieved January 21, 2023, from https://www.dgtelemed.de/downloads/10-Jahre-dgtelemed-web.pdf

Cocchi, R. (2014). *Physician resistance against EHR systems and how to overcome it.* Healthcare Business & Technology.

Cosandey, J., Roten, M., & Rutz, S. (2018). *Gesunde Spitalpolitik.* Retrieved September 12, 2022, from https://www.avenir-suisse.ch/publication/gesunde-spitalpolitik/

Damanpour, F. (1991). Organizational innovation: A meta-analysis of the effects and moderation. *Academy of Management Journal, 34*(3), 555–590.

Dopson, S., Fitzgerald, L., & Ferliec, E. (2008). Understanding change and innovation in healthcare settings: Reconceptualizing the active role of context. *Journal of Change Management, 8*, 213–231.

Drummond, W. H., et al. (2009). Complexity in healthcare information technology systems. In K. Hannah & M. Ball (Eds.), *Health informatics* (2nd ed., pp. 83–118). Springer.

Drucker, P. (2007). *The practice of management (the classic Drucker collection, Rev. ed.).* Butterworth-Heinemann. (original work published in 1955).

Estevez, S., & Cosandey, J. (2022). *Die Spezialisierung von Spitälern vorantreiben.* Retrieved August 23, 2022, from https://www.avenir-suisse.ch/die-spezialisierung-von-spitaelern-vorantreiben

Federal Statistical Office. (2021). *Hospital statistics.* Retrieved August 24, 2022, from https://www.bfs.admin.ch/bfs/de/home/statistiken/gesundheit/erhebungen/ks.html

Fleßa, S. (2018). *Systemisches Krankenhausmanagement.* De Gruyter Oldenburg.

Golder, L., Grez, T., Burgunder, T., & Rey, R. (2021). *Swiss eHealth Barometer 2022: Bericht zur Befragung der Gesundheitsfachpersonen und Akteure des Gesundheitswesens.* Retrieved August 27, 2022, from https://e-healthforum.ch/wp-content/uploads/sites/3/2022/05/223111_Schlussbericht_eHealth_Gesundheitsfachpersonen_V2.pdf

Graetz, F., & Smith, A. C. T. (2010). Managing organizational change: A philosophies of change approach. *Journal of Change Management, 10*, 135–154.

Higgs, M., & Rowland, D. (2000). Building change leadership capability: The quest for change competence. *Journal of Change Management, 1*, 116–130.

Hirschhorn, L. (2002). Campaigning for change. *Harvard Business Review, 80*, 98–104.

Kotter, J. P. (1995). Leading change: Why transformation efforts fail. *Harvard Business Review, 73*, 59–67.

Kotter, J. P. (1996). *Leading change.* Harvard Business School Press.

Kotter, J. P. (2008). *A sense of urgency.* Harvard Business School Press.

Lamothe, L., & Dufour, Y. (2007). Systems of interdependency and core orchestrating themes at health care unit level. A configurational approach. *Public Management Review, 9*(1), 67–85.

Lapointe, L., & Rivard, S. (2006). Getting physicians to accept new information technology: Insights from case studies. *Canadian Medical Association Journal, 174*(11), 1573–1578.

McKinsey. (2021). *Digitization in healthcare: The CHF 8.2 billion opportunity for Switzerland.* Retrieved August 19, 2022, from https://www.mckinsey.com/ch/our-insights/digitization-in-healthcare

Meaney, M., & Pung, C. (2008). McKinsey global results: Creating organizational transformations. *McKinsey Quarterly, August,* 1–7.

Medinside. (2016). *Spital-Bau-Boom in der Schweiz: Ist das noch gesund?* Retrieved August 21, 2022, from https://www.medinside.ch/post/spital-bau-boom-in-der-schweiz-ist-das-noch-gesund

Mintzberg, H. (1980). Structure in 5's: A synthesis of the research on organization design. *Management Science, 26*(3), 322–341.

Nash, D. (1998). Physicians resist efforts to standardize care. *Hospital Case Management, 6*(2), 24–25.

Pepper, A. (2002). Leading professionals: A science, a philosophy and a way of working. *Journal of Change Management, 3*(4), 349–360.

PWC. (2013). *Spitalimmobilien: neue Perspektiven, neue Chancen.* Retrieved August 21, 2022, from https://www.pwc.ch/publications/2016/pwc_spital-immobilien_perspektiven_chancen_d.pdf

Rahimi, K. (2019). Digital health and the elusive quest for savings. *Lancet, 1,* e108–e109.

Rybnicek, R., Bergner, S., & Suk, K. (2016). Führung in Expertenorganisationen. In J. Felfe & R. van Dick (Eds.), *Handbuch Mitarbeiterführung. Wirtschaftspsychologisches Praxiswissen für Fach- und Führungskräfte* (pp. 227–237). Springer.

Sirkin, H., Keenan, P., & Jackson, A. (2005). The hard side of change management. *Harvard Business Review, 83,* 109–118.

Stoddard, J., Hargraves, J., Reed, M., et al. (2001). Managed care, professional autonomy, and income: Effects on physician career satisfaction. *Journal of General Internal Medicine, 16*(10), 675–684.

Synpulse. (2020). *Auf dem Weg zum "digitalen Spital" Marktstudie zum Stand der Digitalisierung in der Schweizer Spitallandschaft.* Retrieved August 25, 2022, from https://www.e-health-suisse.ch/fileadmin/user_upload/Dokumente/D/Studie_Synpulse_Marktstudie_zum_Stand_der_Digitalisierung_in_der_Schweizer_Spitallandschaft.pdf

Thiel, R., et al. (2018). *SmartHealthSystems—International comparison of digital strategies.* Berstelsmann Foundation.

Toedtli, J. (2020). *Klinik-IT Marktübersicht CH-DE 2020.* Retrieved September 2, 2022, from https://www.toedtli-consulting.com/_files/ugd/fdaab8_5bc1d0e8e1b84a43875f5a3f2efdc54c.pdf

Whelan-Berry, K. S., & Somerville, K. A. (2010). Linking change drivers and the organizational change process: A review and synthesis. *J of Change Management, 10,* 175–193.

Widmer, P. (2014). Does prospective payment increase hospital (in)efficiency? Evidem from the Swiss hospital sector. *The European Journal of Health Economics, 16*(4), 407.

Zweifel, P. (2000). Switzerland. *Journal of Health Politics, Policy and Law, 25*(5), 937–944.

Zweifel, P. (2021). Innovation in health care through information technology (IT): The role of incentives. *Social Science and Medicine, 289,* 114441.

Zweifel, P. (2022). Innovation, incentives, and information technology in the healthcare industry. Contributions to economics. In S. Walzer (Ed.), *Digital healthcare in Germany* (pp. 17–31). Springer.

Johannes Schoder is a professor of Health Care Management at the Baden-Wuerttemberg Cooperative State University. His teaching and research focus on health insurance and managed care.

Jan Pieper is a professor of Business Administration at IU International University. His teaching and research focus is on corporate strategy and innovation management.

Philippe K. Widmer is head of corporate development and a board member of a healthcare organization. He is an expert in efficiency measurement and also teaches in this field.

Applying Agile Methodologies in Digital Transformation Processes: Challenges and Lessons Learnt from 10 Years of Consulting Experience

Maddalena D'Aniello

1   Waterfall and Agile methodologies

The possible project methodologies and approaches that can be used to deliver a project vary widely: focusing on the two most commonly used ones, I will investigate the "waterfall" and "agile" methods.[1] Understanding the nature of these two ways of delivery is important for anyone involved in digital transformation, product development, organizational change, program management, or any other kind of structured project. We can begin by outlining the basics of each approach (Fig. 1).

---

[1] Another way to deliver projects is known as "hybrid agile," which combines agile methods with non-agile techniques. Typically, hybrid agile = non-agile ideas + agile concepts, resulting in a mixed approach that takes the best of both worlds. Applying this way of working, implies a high effort when it comes to clarify the real meaning.

M. D'Aniello (✉)
Deloitte Digital, Milan, Italy
e-mail: madaniello@deloitte.it

© The Author(s), under exclusive license to Springer Nature Switzerland AG 2023
C. Hattula, I. Köhler (eds.), *Change Management Revisited*, Business Guides on the Go, https://doi.org/10.1007/978-3-031-30240-4_3

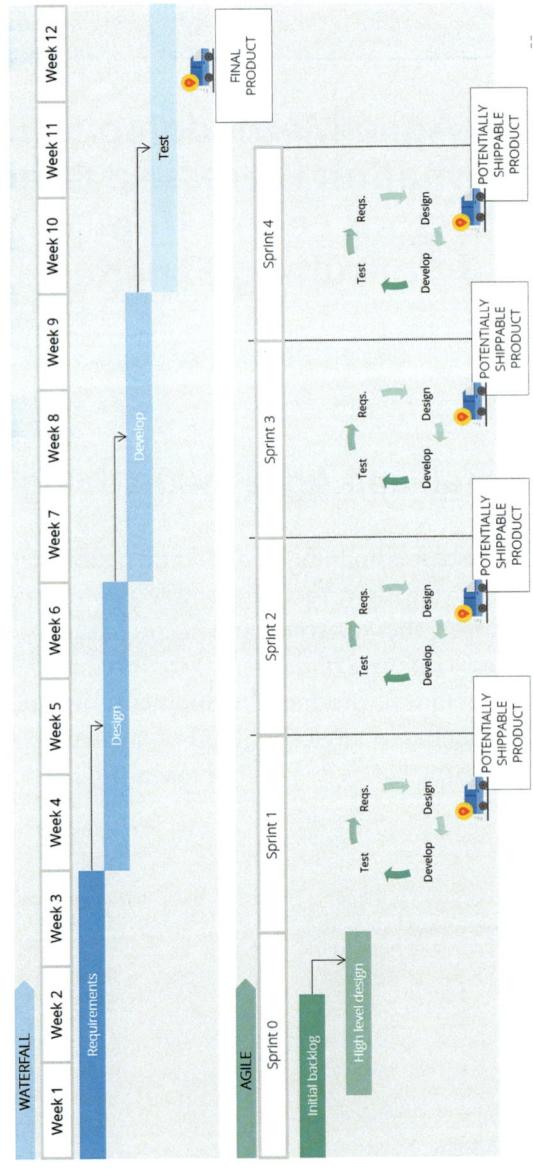

Fig. 1 Key differences between waterfall and agile approaches (own illustration)

Waterfall

The waterfall approach is the traditional way of managing projects. In this methodology, the sequence of events starts with the gathering and documentation of requirements, and then design, code, test (unit test, system test, user acceptance test), fix outstanding issues, and finally deliver the finished product so it can start to be used. This is a mainly linear process, beginning with requirements and ending in a final release or completion of the project, where each stage can start only when the previous one has been completed.

Agile

The agile approach is an iterative and incremental,[2] team-based one that emphasizes the rapid delivery of an application or product in complete functional components. The time is "boxed" into phases called "sprints," which have a defined duration (typically 1–4 weeks) and a list of deliverables, planned at the start of each sprint. Deliverables are prioritized by business value as determined by the customer. If not all the planned work for the sprint can be completed, work is reprioritized. The goal is to deliver value to the customer or user as quickly and often as possible. Thus, larger projects are broken down into smaller chunks so that progress can be made during each sprint. The agile approach was created as a reaction to the waterfall's perceived shortcomings: in 2001, a group of software developers realized that they were collectively developing software in a different way from the traditional waterfall methodology and they created the "Agile Manifesto."[3] A new approach for planning and managing software projects was defined: it puts less

---

[2] Building iteratively means starting with a rough draft and refining further with an increase in details. Building incrementally, one piece at a time, may require the full idea to be formulated. To deep dive: "Don't know what I want, but I know how to get it. Agile Product Design" (Patton, 2008). You can deep dive the topic reading (Darrin & Devereux, 2017; Fowler & Highsmith, 2001; Hazzan & Dubinsky, 2014).

[3] The agile Manifesto is a brief document built on four values and 12 principles for agile software development. The "Agile Manifesto" does not outline any specific processes, procedures, or best practices for agile working. And that is intentional. Its authors did not set out to develop a rigid framework or methodology, but instead created a philosophical mindset that would be useful for software development. For more information on the topic, you can visit the following link https://agilemanifesto.org/

emphasis on up-front plans and strict control and relies more on informal collaboration, coordination, and continuous learning. The agile approach favors discipline in adaptive, continual planning, early delivery, and continual improvement. Most of all it encourages rapid and flexible responses to change.

Now the key question is "Which is the best way to guarantee the success of a project?" There is not one single answer; it depends on the project context.

Waterfall works well, if a project has:

- Clear scope and deliverables
- Customers who are not always available
- A clear goal and solution
- Familiar technology
- Relatively familiar project conditions

Agile works well, if a project has:

- A scope that is not clear in advance.
- A customer available throughout the project.
- Smaller teams with a high degree of coordination and synchronization.
- Time, material, and non-fixed funding.

Over recent years, agile practices have proliferated as a project approach, hence this is this paper's focus. However, these agile practices should not just be followed blindly, but should rather apply to what makes sense in your environment. For this reason, you can apply agile methods in different contexts—digital transformation, organizational change, and business transformation, as well as in the personal sphere (e.g., for wedding planning, moving house, renovating, and so on).

Agile is not something you just do on software.

There is a lot of confusion around agile. It happens frequently that clients ask for a project to be set up using agile methodologies, but they are not prepared on the topic and on its possible impact on their patterns of working in this way: they are unclear as to what exactly it is they are requesting. Some project coordinators may feel that sometimes "agile working" is a trend to follow. It has happened that a team sets down all the project requirements in so-called "user stories," creates an appropriate tool to manage the implementation phase, moves the user stories into this tool, which ends up never being used simply because the implementation team refused to use the tool. In this instance, a project team wasted at least a week of effort on this activity and the client paid for a week's-worth of salaries for a team of four consultants working on activities of zero value. Of course, the chance of failure was on the radar and the team checked several times with the client whether this was the right approach. The answer? "We want to work in Agile. We need user stories."

> Client: "We want to work in Agile." Key questions: What's your "level of agile"? Do you have enough time to dedicate to an "agile project"? Are all the involved teams and resources available to work in agile ways and to use a dedicated tool?

The paper will serve as a guide to successfully set up and manage your next agile-based digital transformation. When it comes to consulting projects, agile does not have one single meaning or one universal framework to apply: in the context of real-world projects, it represents a pathway for adapting project management to client contexts, needs, availability, and levels of expertise in agile maturity. This paper describes learnings and recommendations from three different digital transformation projects,[4] using as examples the typical project phases [5] of an agile-based digital transformation. The project phases considered to support the sharing:

---

[4] Clients' names are anonymous due to non-disclosure agreements.

[5] For further information, see "A Guide to the Project Management Body of Knowledge" (6th Ed., PMBOK Guide).

- Set-up[6]: preparatory activities for starting a new project.
- Execution[7]: daily project activities to create the best possible solution/ service, using an iterative and incremental approach.
- Delivery and roll-out[8]: go live, using the MVPs[9] concept and piloting and testing in a limited geographical or business unit to verify that it works (risk reduction), and then expand the project across the whole company with a clear roll-out strategy.

Story # 1

Story #1 is the story of a digital transformation in a technology, media, and telecom (TMT) company with a customer relationship management (CRM) scope, covering sales, servicing, and "field" service. Its project goals were to increase internal efficiency and improve customer experience. After 10 years of using an old CRM Siebel-based system, it was time to move to a new system based on Salesforce. The project applied a hybrid agile approach in theory—although more similar to the waterfall in practice—but with strong elements of co-design and feedback collection to facilitate implementation and adoption. However, non-predictable external events had a relevant impact on the project timeline.

Set-Up

This project was part of a long and expensive transformation. The team dedicated the right attention to the set-up phase, and the hybrid agile approach was selected to organize the project activities. If "agile" is

---

[6] The set-up phase in digital transformation is a crucial moment for understanding needs and working with clients on how to manage a project, with clear rules, frameworks, governance systems, and templates in place. Each client is different; consultants start sharing a proposal, but a project approach is very similar to a tailored suit.

[7] During the execution phase, you start the daily project activities with the clear goal of creating the final solution/service.

[8] This is the moment when your system/service will be live and will be used by users or customers. In these phases activities are manifold: technical preparation for the time to "go live," training, go live, communication, post go-live support, and adoption monitoring.

[9] MVP stands for minimum viable product. It includes only those features essential and valuable for attracting early-adopter customers and for validating a product idea. It happens sometimes that MVPs are parked and not immediately tested in the market for company constraints (e.g., training or double systems usages)—see "Scrum Guide" (Schwaber & Sutherland, 2017).

sometimes unclear, you can imagine how much vaguer a hybrid approach may be. The absence of common and shared views regarding the approach was the biggest initial challenge of this project—but something more complex and not predictable arrived later.

Learnings to consider:

- Pay attention to setting up the basics and laying the foundations for understanding the value of the activity. The client agreed to the involvement of different users with a high level of involvement in the project (from part-time to fully engaged).
- Avoid wrong and limited communication when it comes to the need to familiarize people with the selected approach and the related framework. Also, if everything was well defined within the core team (made up of clients and consultants)—with the aid of PowerPoint presentations, for instance—they were not clearly communicated outside of the project team to the rest of the company.
- Avoid being agile (or hybrid agile) on paper only. In the end, the project followed a waterfall approach, including a strong element of feedback gathering, rather than a hybrid agile one. The client was not used to working in an agile way. The level of agile readiness was low, so the hybrid agile approach quickly reverted to a more traditional waterfall one. For example, the clients asked for detailed documentation (more than 120 pages to describe a CRM system) to describe requirements with a clear approval process for this long document. A lot of effort was spent in analyzing the document, feedback was gathered, and we only started the implementation phase 2 months later.

Execution

This stage was very complex. The project's scope was extensive, with a large number of project stakeholders and teams involved in different moments. This situation is common, but companies often forget to dedicate time to getting new users on board, to bring them up to speed on approaches and ways of working, or to clearly lay out the timelines, tools, and what had been done until they became involved.

Learnings to consider:

- Focus on what brings you value. Use analytics-driven approaches to processes in order to make best use of resources, timing, operations, and experience. During the project, the team identified the most commonly used processes and activities looking at the data and agreed to simplify removing obsolete and/or little used activites.
- Provide feedback on real and workable system/mockups and not on long document. Work in a responsive and adaptable way. Intensive feedback collection in meetings dedicated to this purpose was adopted to suggest and present improvements to the system.
- In the project "power users" were identified. They had no special power as you can imagine, but they were additional team members involved in the project and they were real system users (call center agents in this case). The purpose of involving them was to collect feedback from actual users: their role was to provide detailed feedback in dedicated sessions but also to be ambassadors for the project. After each meeting to make sure they understood the solution, they had time to be back in their various contact centers located in different locations, explaining and sharing, and providing additional feedback collected from additional real users. This method of collecting feedback was successful and facilitated the system to be successfully adopted.
- Moving from design to system the amount of feedback was too big, creating extra effort for the implementation team. The analysis and design phase prior to the implementation did not involve the right stakeholders.

Delivery and Roll-Out

The delivery and roll-out phases were well organized in this case. Thanks to the introduction of "power users," a wide pool of supporting teams was available in the key moment of this phase: for the training sessions and the first days of the new system go-live.

Learnings to consider:

- Define a clear roll-out strategy, starting with delivering the system first in the internal call center and then to outsourcers, reducing overall project risks.
- Ensure that on-site support is always available in the initial days of go-live to facilitate communication and adoption.
- Due to the project's extensive scope, the company decided to run two active CRM systems (the old one and new one) in parallel. It was not easy to move users onto the new system. At a certain point, it became necessary to force users to work with the new system by blocking access to the previous one. Additionally, even when users recognized the benefits of working with the new system, they continued to use the old one simply because it was easier for them. If possible, avoid using two systems in parallel: at the beginning it will be complex, but in the long term you will see the benefits of this approach.

Change Outcome

All the key performance indicators (KPIs) defined in the initial business case were reached. The agents' productivity increased, the internal net promoter score (NPS) was good, and IT costs were reduced, but the duration of this transformation was too long and one of the main reasons was created by an external and no predictable event.[10] This story is a clear example that it is not possible to predict the unpredictable.

Story #2

Story #2 is related to a company's goal to enter a new market with an e-mobility offer based on a fully digital customer experience. The project goal was to enrich the company proposition based on core business offers, energy and gas, and on adding new complementary services for customers. The core team had extensive expertise in agile ways of working: two members were part of the innovation department and typically these kinds of resources are the most used to agile working, with a completely

---

[10] The company was acquired by the European Group and so they stopped the contract with the system integrator due to independence issues for audit activities. This happened one year after the project started. To restart it was necessary to spend 4 months.

different mindset. This story shows that a good agile core team is not enough if the whole company is not on board with this approach.

Set-Up

This project was small, with a timeline of just 6 months to enter a new market. We dedicated enough time to setting up the project, but this was done inside the core team—seven people representing only three different company departments (innovation, product, and sales). A fully agile approach was adopted but within weeks the problem was clear. When we met the IT team (not part of the core team) to request a small set of capabilities to sell the new offer via existing digital channels, they collected the requests and then after 2 weeks rejected half of the requirements and declared that, following the new IT development process, requirements were unclear and not presented in the right form (or template); they then suggested a first possible date for starting implementation which was at least 3 months later. The original idea had been to launch the commercial offer 2 months before this date. To add complexity, two different consulting companies were part of the core team representing two of the three departments involved.

Learnings to share:

- Ensure a high level of agile readiness in the core team: All the team members were fully aligned on the principles, values, and mindset.
- Approach, framework, and way of working were agreed upon inside the core team, without considering the external company resources. In this case, it was not easy to let them understand key agile concepts like MVPs, iterative, or incremental. Bear in mind that if the entire company is not aligned on the way of working, you will face difficult moments. Could you imagine the impact for developers not ready to receive feedback from business users? They will not have the capacity to manage the improvements collected and on the other side, the agile team will pretend flexibility.

Execution

"Fail fast, fail early, and learn" is part of the agile mindset. It allows you to test, if a product, feature, or service is in line with the market's and internal users' expectations. During the project, this way of working was successfully adopted.

Learnings to share:

- In this phase, the team was fully committed to presenting the new offer in the next annual internal sales meeting. They were forced to strive for simplicity to guarantee the go live and applied the art of increasing the amount of inessential and non-mandatory work they were doing.
- Agile allows you to test and fail fast, but this project featured too many failures. A fragile and complex product was created without any process nor any supporting warranty in place during the delivery. The result was that the product was delivered broken. This happened three times. So clarify the scope of the principle, but keep in mind that failures carry costs for the company.
- The location chosen to test the product was in Sicily. When you have to test something, it is advisable that the location is not so far from you. In this case, it was 1300+ km from the logistics center and it was not possible to be present on-site to see and to ask for feedback: everything was virtual, with a very limited time set aside for contacting customers. Testing without learning represents only a cost for the company.

Delivery and Roll-Out

This project was a clear example of continuous improvement, possible also in the delivery phases. Interviews with real users were planned to collect their views and, based on insights and results gathered from these interviews, suggested improvements were identified and considered during the development of the product.

Learnings to share:

- Be prepared to fail. Having the right mindset to accept suggested improvements is not so common. Accepting that the product, feature, system, or service that you have been working on for months—or even years—is not what markets and users are looking for, is not easy. In this project, after the first months, it was clear that the value proposition was not in line with customers' expectations: the payment model (monthly fee) and the price turned out to be wrong.

- No proper training for the sales team. The product and the related digital services were new for them and very different from what they were used to selling. A new training experience was necessary but for time constraints the existing training process was executed via a virtual webinar. The best product or system in the hands of people unable to use it will be a failure. Keep in mind to train your users in the best possible way.

Change-Related Outcomes

The goal of the transformation was achieved: to enter a new market with a fresh offering, while providing a digital customer experience. This project also generated a great change achievement: the core team was able to show the company the benefits of working in an agile manner. After this transformation, the level of agile expertise increased. The core team continued to work to fine-tune the first offering and a couple of months later, they were able to add further new products and services.

Story #3

This story is about digital transformation in a manufacturing company for the introduction of a new end-to-end CRM (from lead to post-sales support). The plan was for clear ideas on the methodology and approaches to apply; apparently dedicated resources to work on change management (not common for a digital transformation project), but top management was not fully onboarded on the new way of working and on the value of change management. This story is the best one to share the importance of change management in a digital transformation.

Digital experience delivery requires a new way of working and for this reason, a strong component of change management is necessary for several reasons:

- High level of complexity across the organization.
- Organizational impacts: new job roles, skills, and behaviors.
- A new customer experience and a new way of interacting with customers.
- A new company culture, if you decide to work in a different way (e.g., working in agile).

Working only on design, processes, integration, and technology is not enough if you do not properly set up change management, with dedicated resources involved to support the stream. It seems obvious but it is far from it.

Learnings to share:

- Give attention to the set-up phase, including the need for company alignment on methodology, terminology, and approach.
- Keep in mind the importance of change management. In this case, the team asked for dedicated training sessions on the selected approach to allow the company to have a common starting point and avoid misunderstandings. Different sessions for different users were planned: one for stakeholders, one for product owners, one for middle management, and one for top management. But this happened too late, months after the project had started.
- Agile requires more time and effort than traditional approaches. The effort of the internal resources was not well defined. Capacity of the resources involved was not verified, which resulted in people working over capacity, creating frustration inside the team.

Execution

Flexibility is not easy to manage working with consultants in the implementation activities. Continuous feedback collection is an easy principle to understand but managing the amount of feedback that you may receive is something complex to manage if it is not foreseen in the planning. Contract constraints and parameters should always be borne in mind when you're designing a project approach.

Learnings to share:

- A working software is the primary measure of progress. All the team was committed to this goal and so they accepted a trade-off: business users were flexible in terms of accepting different solutions from what had originally been designed.
- Flexibility will be limited if you do not plan for changes in advance. Keep in mind your desired way of working so that contracts can be drawn up that are in line with the requested approach. For example, add a few working days to cover changes in schedule or budget.

Delivery and Roll-Out

Identifying where to start with the delivery of the transformation is vital. You will need to find a region, a country, or a marketplace that is prepared to accept the risks associated with being the first. But also, to consider that as first, they can expect to receive greater support.

Learnings to share:

- Put in place an effective roll-out strategy with a clear principle to test every product increment in a selected country, and then continue the roll-out across the rest of the region.
- A train-the-trainer approach was adopted, so this means that internal trainers 2 months before go-live, started to work on the review of the training materials. Keep in mind to involve them from the beginning: they need to have control of the content to better explain the content to end users.

Change Outcome

This transformation is on-going. Learnings will be shared in the next book. As of today, the biggest success in this case has been the introduction of a new way of working. After initial resistance in the set-up phase and along the path to achieve the initial MVP, the team approached the transformation in the right way and with the right mindset.

2   Final Retrospective

This paper concludes with a suggested recipe to effectively manage digital transformation in an agile way.

> **Ten Suggestions from Maddalena**
>
> - Dedicate attention to your set-up phase.
> - Adapt agile fundamentals to your company and to your needs and possibility.
> - Use what you need: your project does not have to be 100% agile.
> - Familiarize (or socialize) relevant teams and managers with the project approach you have defined with the operative team and top management.
> - If a training session on agile is necessary, do not hesitate to plan it.
> - Contracts with third parties and the project approach need to be aligned.
> - Agile is not easy: it may require more discipline than more traditional approaches.
> - Do not forget to include change-management activities.
> - Keep in mind that change management is not only training, but also includes examining organizational impact, communication, and adoption monitoring.
> - Flexibility: above all means having a flexible mind.
>
> And one last suggestion: have fun with your next agile project!

References

Darrin, M., & Devereux, W. (2017). *The agile manifesto, design thinking and systems engineering.* In 11th Annual IEEE International Systems Conference.

Fowler, M., & Highsmith, J. (2001). The agile manifesto. *Software Development Magazine, 9*(8), 29–30.

Hazzan, O., & Dubinsky, Y. (2014). The agile manifesto. In *Agile anywhere: Essays on agile products and beyond* (pp. 1–2). Springer.

Patton, J. (2008). *Don't know what I want, but I know how to get it.* Agile Product Design. Retrieved January 21, 2023, from https://www.jpattonassociates.com/dont_know_what_i_want/

Schwaber, K., & Sutherland, J. (2017). *Scrum guide.* Retrieved January 21, 2023, from www.scrum.org

Maddalena D'Aniello is a senior manager at Deloitte Digital, a consulting company in Italy specializing in supporting clients to manage successful digital transformation. She is Italian and based in Milan but originally from Caserta. Maddalena has worked in various industries (TMT, travel & leisure, energy, resources and industrial, manufacturing, consumer), focusing on different types of transformation (CRM, product development and go-to-market, new channels introduction/replacement—e.g., new chat and pricing digitalization), across different locations (in her home country as well as internationally) and with a variety of stakeholders (operative project core team, middle management, and top management). In line with her professional career, she has had different project roles depending on the kinds of digital transformation undertaken by firms she has worked for: she started as a business consultant supporting business users in their analysis, concentrating on company requirements and design activities, and then became an Agile Coach and SCRUM Master to facilitate the adoption of agile methodologies, which led to her roles as an expert in business transformation and eventually as a project manager tasked with delivering excellence. Summarizing her professional capabilities, she can help clients to change starting from the introduction of a new technology and a digital experience but also guide them in a new way of working that applies a new mindset. As a certified SCRUM Master, she uses agile-oriented management principles to organize digital transformation. Internally, she is helping her company to enhance its approaches to diversity, inclusion, and equality, working as an ambassador for these important topics.

From Input to Outcomes: Bayer's Digital Transformation of Agricultural Business Exploration

Arnd Nenstiel-Köhling and Josef H. Exler

1 Introduction: The Rationale for a Strategic Review

Traditionally, the crop protection industry's business model is largely based on charging farmers for chemical solutions to solve agronomic problems in the field. Business growth is driven by increases in volume and by the replacement of off-patent/generic chemistry with IP-protected chemistry that tends to be more expensive but more effective. The incentive for any input company to achieve the targets for its respective chemistry portfolio lies in driving volume growth with average per-hectare use rates as part of the product range.

Digital technologies have disrupted many established industries, leading to them exploring innovative, more efficient, and more convenient

---

Arnd Nenstiel-Köhling and Josef Exler contributed equally with all other contributors.

A. Nenstiel-Köhling (✉) • J. H. Exler (✉)
Bayer AG, Leverkusen, Germany
e-mail: arnd.nenstiel@bayer.com; josef.exler@bayer.com

ways to meet customer needs (as an example, e-mails have superseded much of the traditional communication by post). However, the increasing adoption of digital tools in agriculture should not be viewed as a mere add-on to the chemical crop protection market by the augmentation of physical products (such as using digital marketplaces or digital marking tools that recommend the purchase of physical products). Digital tools collecting sub-field-specific information and translation of these into actionable insights will instead become a driver of innovative, digitally enabled, agronomy-focused business models. Taking as an example, the weed problem faced by a farmer: field crops compete with weeds for water, sunlight, and nutrition. To protect their harvests, farmers may be using a particular chemical-based herbicide (mixture), applying this at the same time—with a specific and registered dose rate—to the entire field to protect the crop and control weeds, independent of the weeds' distribution, density, and species.

In future, digital technology will be used to replace such "one size fits all" solutions with those tailored to the specific needs of each field, to an accuracy measured in square meters. Sub-field-specific insights will be created based on high-resolution images captured with high geospatial accuracy. These images will be analyzed by algorithms to differentiate crops from weeds, thus becoming actionable by translating the geospatial information of the weeds' locations into precise application maps, which can then be used for much more closely targeted treatment with herbicides. Applying the chemical product in a precise way just on those areas of the field where the agronomic problem—in this case, weed infestation—is present translates to a volume saving of the chemical product. Furthermore, the gathering of such high-resolution imagery will open the door for even more agronomy focused and tailored products.

Alongside the growth of digital technologies comes the increase in public pressure regarding the environmental impact of crop protection products. Equally, established providers of agricultural equipment (particularly with regard to precision application technology) as well as newer start-ups have not been shy in challenging the existing crop protection market dominated by traditional players in the crop protection market. For example, in 2022 John Deere, a farm equipment manufacturing giant, introduced the See & Spray™ Ultimate precision application sprayer to the US market. Alongside the firm's role as a provider of precision application technology, it is now claiming to achieve a substantial reduction in the volume of chemical crop protection products for clients using their technology. The resultant savings for their customers (farmers) is intended to be shared with the provider(s) of the hardware and software.

Consequently, for Bayer, there is a substantial risk of losing out on the "last mile" (in other words, a product's actual application by growers). This means a high value at stake: a substantial volume reduction of chemistry used could potentially mean a sales loss of several billion euros for Bayer's crop protection weed management business alone.

Against this backdrop, Bayer teams are even now embarked on an intensive strategy review and change program to (a) quantify the shifts in value pools accessible to the company in the future, and (b) to drive new ventures that will help to capture value.

2   Methodology: Quantifying the Need for Change and the Opportunities

We first needed to make the case for change (using the Prosci ADKAR model, 2022: Awareness, Desire, Knowledge, Ability, Reinforcement) and to pave the way for robust decision-making approaches relating to the changes needed within the Bayer organization. It was therefore decided to initially build a *market model*, simulating and quantifying the anticipated changes in value per segment and to then address the prerequisites that would enable changes to these segments to be accessed.

At the outset, the project team working on the strategic review and the subsequent strategic initiatives to drive the change formulated a mission statement:

> We need to move from selling a single physical product (via various levels of distribution) to offering a solution, including the service (working title: "weed controlled field"). This should include the last step of application. Solely enhancing the product offering via an algorithm (i.e. weed control recommendation alone) will not be sufficient. Essentially, we are talking about an end-to-end business offering to our grower customers.

2.1   A Quantitative Market Model to Support the Case for Change

The team first identified key qualitative market trends—based on a range of factors, such as regulatory and agronomic needs, competitors' innovation pipelines, and sustainability aspects—impacting the market segment for chemical weed control. Those qualitative trends were then captured and quantified (via expert interviews, market research data, and workshops) for the top 20 markets for weed control, amounting to roughly 80% of the global market value. Taking this approach focused the research and gave the authors time to understand and simulate the previously mentioned market trends in each of the top 20 geographical sub-markets.

The market model was built along three dimensions which can be seen in Fig. 1.

(a) *Customer Pain Point*

Every value-adding product is designed to solve the problem of a specific customer group. To ensure customer focus, our project

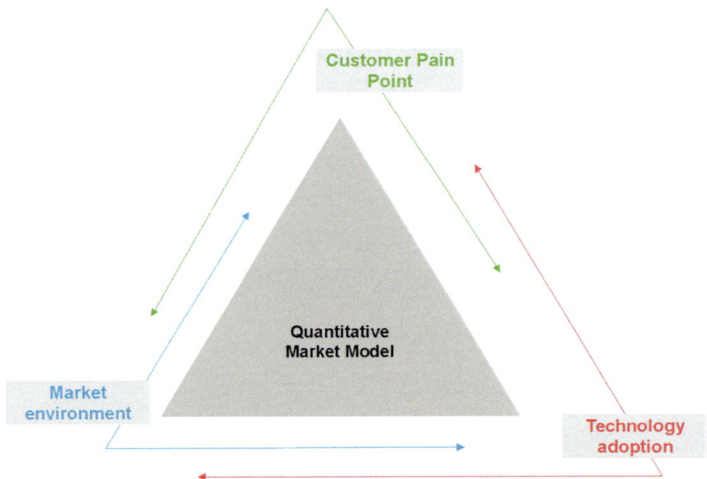

Fig. 1 Impact factors quantified for a market model analyzing the need for change. (Exler & Nenstiel-Köhling, 2022)

started with an internal team of Bayer's agronomic experts mapping out today's pain points for farmers (particular weeds that are difficult to control, and the status of resistance against established chemical herbicides, for example). Building on these aspects, the team also identified future needs and upcoming opportunities for digital technologies (like computer-assisted scouting and the use of drones).

(b) *Technology development and adoption*

The latest development of digitally enabled precision application technologies was closely tracked and monitored, based mainly on the publicly available communications of technology providers, trade shows, and expert interviews. According to the "diffusion of innovations" model (Rogers, 2003) the adoption of any innovation in a social system can be viewed as a pattern of diffusion. The diffusion in any customer group (in this case, farmers) gains momentum after the first, so-called "innovators" have started using a new technology (for example, tractors that can be steered automatically). These pioneers are followed by "early adopters," an "early majority," the "late majority," and culminating with "laggards." Plotting the relative adoption against time leads to the familiar S-shaped adoption curves. In the light of uncertainties regarding the adoption of digitally enabled precision application technologies over a 10-year time period, our market model examined three distinct scenarios with different S-curves (relating to slow, medium, and fast adoption).

(c) *Market environment*

Alongside technologies and customer needs, the broader market environment is also changing, especially in a regulated market like agrochemicals. To quantify the future impact on markets, chemical scientists, and regulatory experts took a close look at changes in the firm's external environment, in this case the proliferation of resistant weeds and regulatory frameworks in key market geographies around the world.

The quantified market model as an outcome of the previously described steps then formed the basis for identifying shifts in Bayer's weed management strategy.

2.2 Empirical Business Model Innovation: "Test and Learn" with Real Customers

As outlined in the mission statement for the strategic review and with the insights gleaned from the market model, it became apparent that a new approach to innovation and market exploration was needed. In the context of an established company such as Bayer, which has accumulated decades of experience with the technologies pertinent to incremental innovation within its core market and has gained comprehensive knowledge of its present-day customers, conventional methods of problem-solving typically involve a project-based approach utilizing a linear and static "waterfall" methodology, which encompasses a project plan, milestones, and Gantt charts, among other features. Given the uncertainty about the details regarding which digital technologies will ultimately prevail in the agricultural setting (drone-based field imagery vs. tractor-mounted cameras, or computing on a device vs. in the cloud) and the high degree of uncertainty surrounding future customer requirements (e.g., the relative lack of detail about implementation of the EU's Green Deal[1]) an agile approach was chosen instead, with the team knowing that this would require organizational change (ref. Fig. 2; Stacey, 2000).

To put into practice the principles of agile product development (Beck et al., 2001) within a process-driven corporate culture, some key aspects needed to be considered. Against the backdrop of the overarching aim to satisfy the customer, a shift from processes to individual interaction and accountability is necessary (Beck et al., 2001). This accountability calls for empowerment and ownership of the problem. Instead of a PMO (project management officer) carrying out a fixed and time-boxed project plan aligned with multiple stakeholders, a "product owner" is needed. The role could be better described as being taken by a "problem owner" who would ideally understand a customer's problem in depth but who would not be the driving force behind a plan. They would instead be

---

[1] The EU Green Deal, announced by the European Commission in December 2019, comprises a set of policies and regulatory decisions to transform the EU27 economy toward net-zero carbon emissions by 2050. This set of policies and regulations will give rise to significant impacts and implications for agri-input providers and their customers (for example, by restricting access to crop protection solutions and fertilizer spreading).

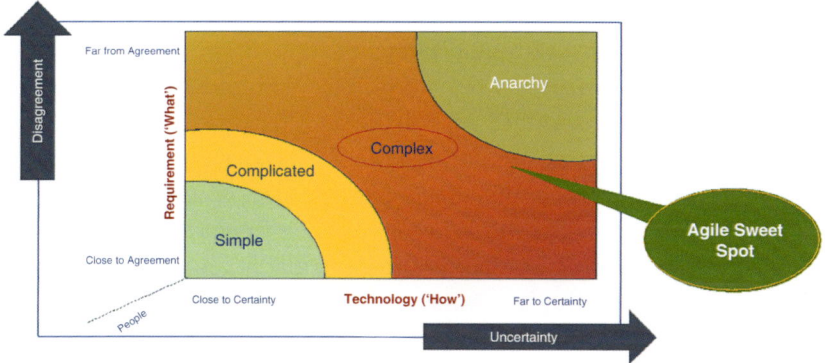

Fig. 2 Adopted Stacey matrix (Stacey, 2000)

working iteratively on a solution to that specific problem, while perhaps even working against the overall vision. With the customer as the focus, development of minimal viable products (MVPs) that can be tested at an early stage directly with farmers is the goal, rather than coming up with perfectly designed, holistic, and complex solutions with prolonged development timelines. Therefore, we should value adoption and iterative change based on empirical customer feedback rather than clinging to a slavish adherence to fixed milestone-based planning (Beck et al., 2001).

To establish this new culture and manage the ambiguity of the different markets, we finally set up two regional business ventures, led by dedicated and empowered "venture leads"—in other words, product owners—covering two of the most relevant (as quantified in the market model) and agronomically different geographies.

2.3 Core Business Changes and Stakeholder Activation

As part of the third aspect of our process of change, the project team focused on Bayer's internal stakeholders and how to identify the changing needs of our established core businesses.

To foster the desire for and ownership of change, we invited more than 40 Bayer experts from different core functions to a 2-day workshop, thus ensuring a broad perspective with a truly global footprint (R & D, Sales, Marketing, Product Supply, and Finance).

The workshop pursued two main objectives: understanding our competitors' (likely) approaches to enhancing their customer offerings in weed management, and simulating potential strategic moves on the part of these companies that could affect Bayer's future success in this segment.

The second part of this workshop proved to generate particularly valuable insights for testing our new strategy against potential moves of competitors and for building a common awareness of the need for change for our entire industry.

Implications for the core business that were identified (for example, refocusing R & D) were later communicated internally—in the form of a "strategy house" (see Fig. 3)—to the Executive Leadership team of the company.

Practice Tip

Senior leadership endorsement with dedicated resources to start experimenting is a key to success; leaving established processes and decision pathways requires a clear vision but should be based at the same time on a wide-ranging freedom to operate. This needs to be clear from the beginning.

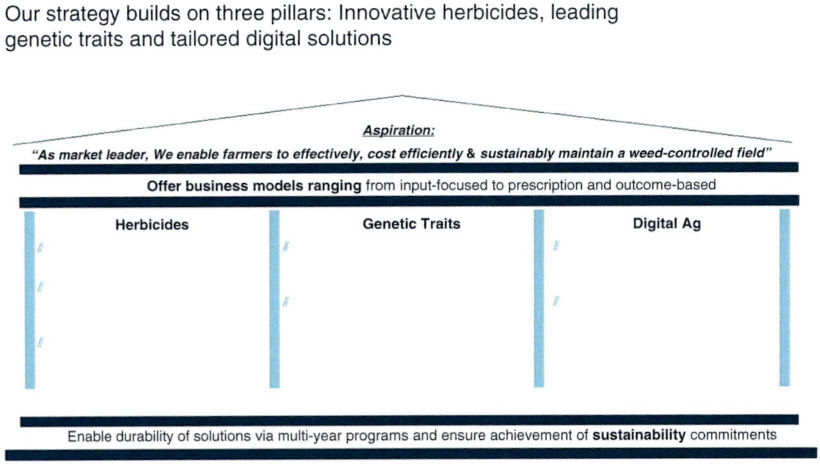

Our strategy builds on three pillars: Innovative herbicides, leading genetic traits and tailored digital solutions

Fig. 3 Streamlined version of the "strategy house" used for internal communications relating to change (Exler & Nenstiel-Köhling, 2022)

3   Reflections and Key Lessons Learnt

Our real-life experience matches well with what Clayton Christensen called the "innovator's dilemma" (Christensen, 1997). When business models change, established players are structurally handicapped. In a large corporate organization, every project is competing with a host of alternative options for internal resources. For incremental, sustainable innovation the probability of success and the potential for value generation are typically estimated on the basis of years (or decades) of experience.

Yet, the opposite applies to disruptive innovations or new business models. If the targeted market does not yet exist, there is little chance for companies to build a reliable business case based on the widely used criterion of net present value (NPV). However, without a reliable business case it is a tough call to ask a portfolio committee for funding, especially as disruptive concepts tend to be competing with incremental and innovative projects that can (or pretend to) precisely project annual top- and bottom-line contributions. For disruptive or new business models only market or value potential can be anticipated and quantified. The intrinsic conflict between short-term bottom-line optimization and long-term top-line enablement becomes apparent, when an established and profitable product is faced with being cannibalized by a disruptive concept with an initially lower margin—but with perhaps a greater long-term business potential.

Taking as an example an established automotive company to illustrate this conflict: although the firm's managers are aware of future regulation on air pollution and carbon taxation that will require significant changes in its product portfolio, they may view a short-term "facelift" of an established—and thus usually mass produced—model using a combustion engine is seen as a more value-creating option, indicated by a higher NPV. The alternative and disruptive new electric model is burdened with initially higher manufacturing costs at low output figures—translating into a lower product margin. For an established player, destroying or devaluing a well-established business amount to "biting the hand that feeds you." On the other hand, if there are untapped inefficiencies in the market, it is just a question of time until other players succeed in identifying and exploiting these openings. And this is generally when new players enter the scene. Coming fresh to the stage, there is literally nothing they can lose; every euro or dollar they make is incremental and there are no margin expectations to be met. On top of that, there are no established processes and hardly any internal alignment costs, so new entrants can focus fully on solving customer problems and can aggressively grow the top line to develop and claim the new market. We all know the name of a company that did exactly that, going from a standing start to becoming the market's—if not the world's—most valued car manufacturer in less than 20 years.

Our market model served as a bridge for our Crop Science organization. Although the project team could not provide a full business model with an accompanying NPV, our quantitative model proved to be invaluable for an organization like Bayer, with its decades of expertise in number-driven decision-making. The model was instrumental in generating knowledge about the extent of future opportunities and the desire among staff for change. Being able to clearly articulate the size of a new value pool has paved the way for greater involvement and engagement on the part of leadership and organizational stakeholders.

But to reiterate, we should not underestimate our inability to immediately articulate what a future value-capture model could look like and how a new venture might perform against the established business, relative to return on investment. This is a challenge beyond those presented by annual investment decisions and budgeting tasks and will need to be addressed continuously.

Another lesson we learnt was that the complex nature of the industry's transformation requires a marked degree of ownership and exposure to the technical challenges customers are facing. "Test and learn," with internal teams "owning" a problem and working, literally in the field, on customer issues is an essential prerequisite for an in-depth understanding of the solution space. This know-how cannot be acquired in the form of external advice or analyzed merely by sitting at a desk.

Furthermore, large organizations are usually good at managing complex networks of internal stakeholders. This complexity is needed to run a cross-regional, multi-product business. To maintain their remit on customers' problems, agile teams need a strong external focus. This creates conflicts when it comes to aligning interests with those of internal actors, such as middle management, or with specific departments (covering IT or marketing, for example). Therefore, (re-)defining the organizational and structural set-up is another key success factor we identified. "Insulated but not isolated" is a principle we applied (Pisano, 2019). Placing the venture teams in a protected environment "at arm's length" and minimizing access by the rest of the organization to the agile team within these incubators seemed to have been instrumental to the ventures' success. What seems to be essential ingredients in this success are clear communication and expectation management by the team, and definitive support from top management to keep the project's focus on customers. Another key factor is an incubatory framework for the team's activities that limits the risk of distraction by too much involvement from stakeholders, both internal and external.

Practice Tips

- Value customers first, returns on your investment second. If you identify the right problem and your solution is value adding for the customer, this will open a path to value creation.
- Do not quantify the unknown unknowns. Evaluate overall (new) value opportunities instead of trying to build overly detailed business cases for products that do not exist in markets that are as yet undeveloped.
- Disrupting your established business model calls for fresh thinking. To explore untapped opportunities, use talents with entrepreneurial (or "intra-preneurial") mindsets that focus on people rather than processes.
- Define and devise the right organizational set-up. New ideas need to grow and be nurtured. Encapsulate or insulate the transformative unit at arm's length from the core organization. Actively manage interfaces with corporate/business functions. Keep team focus on customers' problems instead of on stakeholder management.

References

Beck, K., et al. (2001). *Manifesto for agile software development.* Retrieved January 21, 2023, from https://agilemanifesto.org/

Christensen, C. M. (1997). *Innovator's dilemma: when new technologies cause great firms to fail* (Management of innovation and change). *Harvard Business Review Press.*

Deere, J. (2022). *Press release on company website 2022-03-03* (pp. 11–14). Retrieved January 21, 2023, from https://www.deere.com/en/news/all-news/see-spray-ultimate/

Exler, J. H., & Nenstiel-Köhling, A. (2022). Bayer internal report. 2022.

Pisano, G. P. (2019). The hard truth about innovative cultures. *Harvard Business Review, 01*(02), 2019.

Prosci. (2022). *The Prosci ADKAR model.* Retrieved January 21, 2023, from https://www.prosci.com/methodology/adkar

Rogers, E. M. (2003). *Diffusion of innovations* (5th ed.). Free Press.

Stacey, R. D. (2000). Strategic management and organization dynamics. In *The challenge of complexity.* Pearson Education.

Arnd Nenstiel-Köhling Between 2018 and 2022 Arnd led Strategic Marketing and Portfolio Management for Bayer's Crop Protection Herbicides portfolio as Global Head of Asset Management Herbicides. Within this role, he defined the transformational/change roadmap ("from Volume to Value") and strategy for Bayer's weed management portfolio across Seeds & Traits, Crop Protection, and Digital/Precision Application technology to guide Research and Development, Investment, Portfolio, and Production Capacity decisions for the company in these areas.

Arnd started his career at Bayer's Crop Science division in 2003 as a Global Product Manager. He subsequently spent five years in Asia, where—among various roles—he was the Country Commercial Lead of the Crop Science division in Vietnam. After returning to his home country of Germany, he oversaw global Customer Relationship Management activities as part of the company's Global Marketing arm and has also been in charge of the Public Affairs department of the division globally.

Arnd graduated from the University of Applied Sciences in Essen, subsequently received a Master of Business Administration degree from IE Business School in Madrid, and was awarded a Master of Laws (LLM) degree by the University of Münster. He also has a PhD in Agricultural Economics, from the University of Rostock.

Josef H. Exler, is an innovation enthusiast who has spent more than 10 years with Bayer in a variety of roles focusing on innovation. Translating technically driven improvements into business opportunities is one of his main motivations, whether as a Portfolio Analyst, Market Intelligence Manager, or Lead for New Weed Control Technologies. Since 2019, Josef has been one of the driving forces behind the transformation of Bayer's business model for weed management. And in 2021 he joined Bayer's transformative Digital Farming Innovation Lab as Head of Growth & Digital Weed Management Strategy.

With his scientific background in the life sciences, an MSc in Biochemistry from the Technical University of Munich and a PhD from the University of Regensburg, and his expertise in agile product work (as a "Scrum Master") he is an impassioned advocate for the continuous refinement of quantitative and empirical methods to help enhance business effectiveness.

Part II

Cultural and Organizational Transformation Processes

Digital Transformation Within a Large Logistic Company: From a Hierarchical Technocracy into Networked, Agile Teams

Laetitia Henriot Arsever

1 Introduction to the Change Project, Settings, and Goals, Description of the Digital Product/Software/ Solution Introduced

Digital transformation is part of many companies' strategies. While it relies on new technologies such as Cloud, AI, or IOT, and a good enterprise architecture, the right technology stack and top software development and engineering are essentials, though clearly not sufficient. According to an array of consultants (including Forbes, McKinsey, and BCG), over 70% of digital transformation fails (Block, 2002). Digital transformation's success is highly dependent on the human factor. Therefore, it is critical that organizational, business and IT departments look at their operating models, cultures, and leadership and how they can more effectively support the new needs of a world increasingly marked by VUCA (volatility, uncertainty, complexity, and ambiguity).

L. H. Arsever (✉)
Valora Holding AG, Muttenz, Switzerland

With this in mind, I would like to share the experience I made lately, the successes, failures, and lessons I have learnt while being responsible for the strategy, enterprise architecture, program management, and steering of the digital transformation of a rather traditional company.

When I started working, the new strategy had only recently been redefined and approved with the ambition of growing the company. While services were mainly delivered in the physical world, demand for the most profitable services was in constant decline, as were revenue and overall profitability. The strategy was to compensate with efficiency, automatization, and digitalization of current processes and in addition create new digital services. The goal was to leverage the current value proposition and translate it into the digital world so that the company would remain a key player as a public service provider in the future. The idea was also to provide services that would be manifest across the physical and digital world as a continuum. We called it "phygital" services. To deliver this growth strategy, it was clear that the company's IT division (with its more than 1700 staff) would play an important role in ensuring that the necessary capabilities were available.

While defining critical projects and programs, it became clear that the main challenges were less about technology and architectural changes (Cloud, CI/CD, data-driven architecture, Zero Trust, etc.) and more about our operating model, processes, structures, culture, and leadership. As Head of Technology, Strategy, and Steering at the IT division, I identified the same need within my team of 60 and decided to experiment with some fairly radical ideas regarding our operating model, at least for a state owned, traditional, and patriarchal company. I wanted to move from a top-down organization and a "command and control" style of leadership to a more agile, self-organized model and toward more visionary and servant-oriented types of leadership. These are the objectives we set for our transformation:

We increase our impact and transparency to maximize our value generation:

- By involving the concerned roles and units and making them part of our structure and decision-making.
- By empowering employees to become more autonomous, accountable, and to operate as equal partners.

- By increasing the quality of our decisions.
- By making clear, timely, and appropriate decisions.
- By cultivating and living a culture of equity.

We increase our adaptability:

- By responding proactively and quickly to technological and structural changes in our environment.

We increase the employability of our staff:

- By making employees more responsible, engaged, connected, and entrepreneurial.
- By providing an environment in which each employee can develop independently.

We increase our efficiency:

- By using swarm intelligence.
- By clearly assigning competences to specific roles.

In order to achieve these, we used an open framework called Sociocracy 3.0|Effective Collaboration At Any Scale (sociocracy30.org). I chose this framework because I wanted to push for more agility and needed a framework that would support teams that were not project-, program-, or product-oriented. It is based on the well-known "holacracy" model that has been tested in many companies while addressing several pain points (Bernstein et al., 2016). It is the next generation of self-organized teams that is more modular and balances top-down and bottom-up approaches. In particular, I liked that it is a toolbox where you do not have to do it all or nothing but one that enables you to select what is relevant and most impactful for your organization. It is open source and encourages you to experiment with it and adapt it to your own particularities. I found it in that sense not dogmatic but pragmatic. The framework addresses the need to think beyond the mentality of "my" or "your" team, gives flexibility and allows you to include people outside your direct reports when needed.

In this framework, we selected some tools, canvases, and processes and then adapted these to our needs, priorities, and culture.

After understanding and communicating the drivers for our transformation, we started by defining "domains" or "circles." Domains are distinct areas of responsibility and autonomy and we aimed to align them with value creation for our colleagues and partners. What was important in our process was that we separated this discussion from one about the headcounts assignment to the domain identification. This separation was possible because people would not just report to a superior but would work on a topic to create an impact. It could therefore be likely that someone is working on multiple topics and teams. We then defined roles that were needed for each domain. Here too, roles were defined independently of the people and someone could very well be assuming different roles within a domain or across several domains. Figures 1, 2, and 3 give an overview of the domains (which we called circles) and roles we defined.

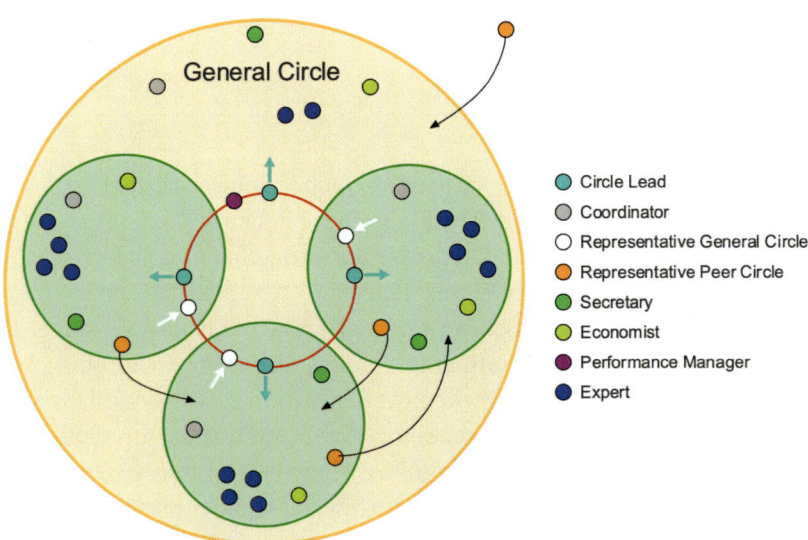

Fig. 1 Roles and circles

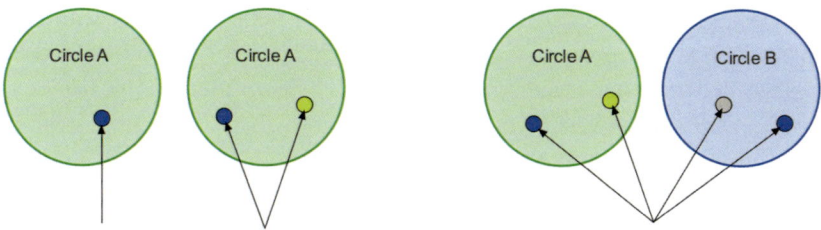

Fig. 2 Employee working options (1 – *n* domains and 1 – *n* roles)

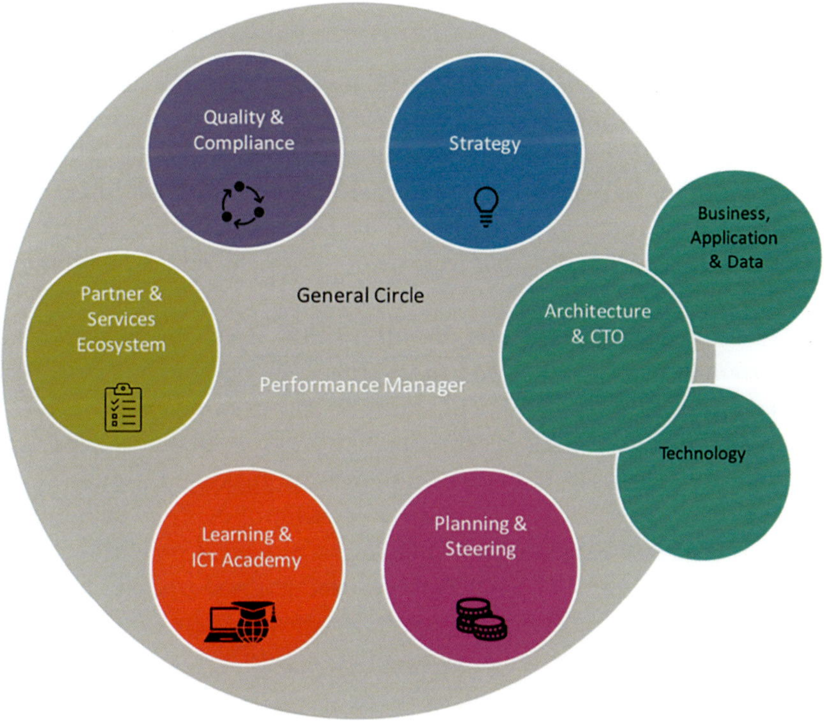

Fig. 3 Organizational domains/circles—an example

In this model, we decided to split the functional and line reporting. All employees would report to the performance manager role as line reporting (see appendix for more details on the roles we defined). That allowed us more flexibility by easily being able to focus our efforts on one topic or another without constantly having to transfer people to other teams. The discussion was more on what we, as a team, needed to deliver and how best to achieve that rather than having each team identifying topics and tasks to optimize their own resources. In addition, we ensured everyone was fully dedicated to the learning, development, and performance of each employee. The performance manager did not have to prioritize between spending time pushing a topic or developing a person. You can see below the sorts of interaction that occurred between the performance manager, the functional lead, and the employees (Fig. 4).

Decision-Making

Before this framework was introduced, decisions were made in two possible ways, sometimes in a top-down manner, where it is often a single person who makes the call but risks not getting true buy-in or could be ignoring other important facts. Alternatively, and more often than not, decisions were made by consensus, meaning everybody needed to agree with the decision to be able to move on, which took a long time to achieve.

We wanted to have the best of both worlds: speed and buy-in. So for important decisions we started to use the "consent" method. Decisions are taken by all impacted people and are approved not when everyone agrees but when no valid objection remains. This helped us move toward "good enough and safe enough to try" decision-making. Introducing this process leads to a shift away from the supremacy of personal opinions and toward more fact-based decision-making. It also gives weight to the person proposing instead of the person criticizing. I find it useful because it helps to remove these emotional tensions and discussions and allows you to make timely decisions that have strong buy-in.

Objectives

We also introduced a quarterly "rhythm" to define objectives and move toward OKRs[1] (objectives and key results), allowing us to further focus

---

[1] OKRs, or "objectives and key results," is a collaborative goal-setting methodology used by teams and individuals to set challenging, ambitious goals with measurable results. OKRs reflect how you

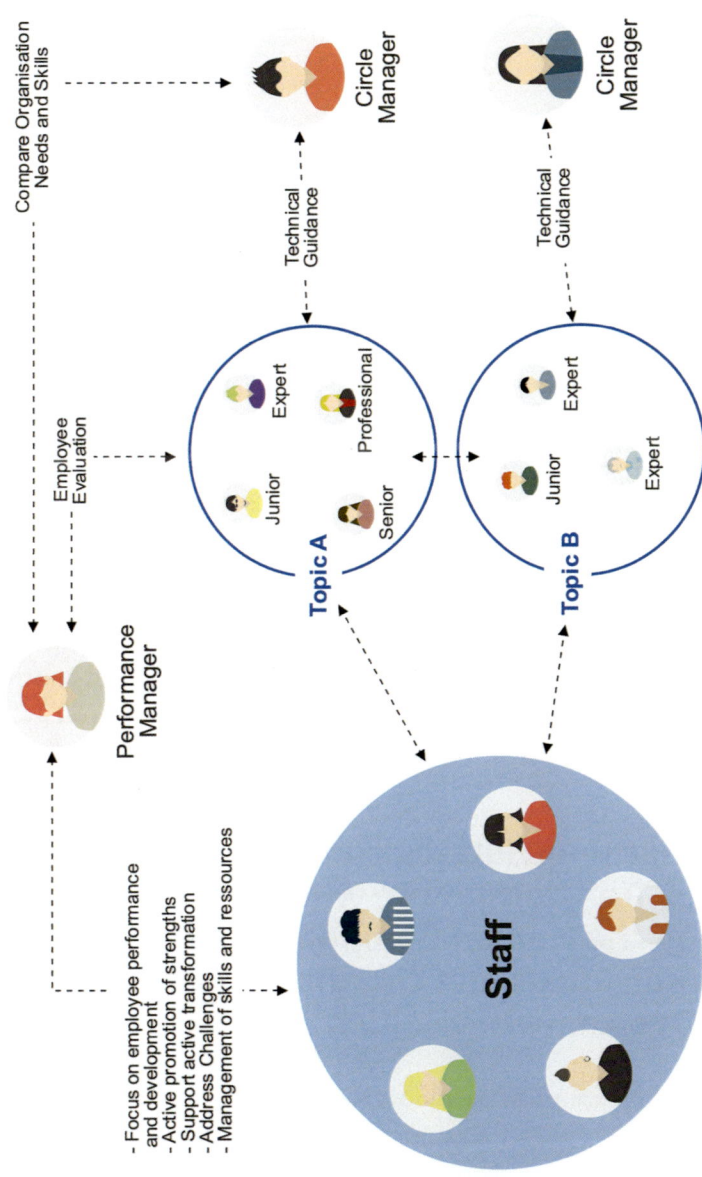

Fig. 4 The performance manager role, the organization, and people development

on impact and value generation. Those shorter cycles made us more adaptable.

Transparency

Finally, I would like to mention an important element: transparency. While we gave more autonomy and delegated more decision-making power within the organization, we always balanced it with more transparency. We ensured this by first agreeing as to the platform on which information would be stored. And we had as a policy that all our documentation, objectives, drafts, discussions, chats, protocols, and agendas would be accessible to everyone across the organization. The only exception would be personal data (related to salary or health, for instance). We also used Kanbans[2] that were linked to this so it would be easy for anyone to find out who was working on what.

Other Elements

With time, we also introduced other elements (feedback, peer review, 360° evaluation, calling meetings to smooth out tensions, the introduction of buddy onboarding, and a happiness officer, for example) based on continuous learning and input from everyone in the various teams.

2   Learnings/Pitfalls on the Path to Transformation, with a Focus on the Human Component, and How Individuals and Organizations Overcame Difficulties

There were four groups of people or roles affected by the changes we made:

---

track progress, create alignment, and encourage engagement around measurable goals.

[2] This approach aims to "manage work by balancing demands with available capacity, and by improving the handling of system-level bottlenecks." https://en.wikipedia.org/wiki/Kanban_(development)

- Employees as single contributors
- Former middle managers of direct employees
- Managers of managers
- Other people interacting with the team

Single Contributors

For a single contributor, working in a "sociocratic" organization means taking on more responsibility and initiative. They have more freedom and opportunities to make decisions, own, and influence how work is done and influence tactical and operational direction. This increase in autonomy and responsibilities is often welcomed but can also create uncertainty.

Some were used to being assigned clear tasks, deadlines, instructions, and priorities. They were usually asked to get approval from their superior for all decisions. They were expected to report to their superior as soon as they encountered a problem, blockage, or difficulty, and in return expected the latter to resolve issues. Many had been working for years on the basis of this model and either did not know how to work in a different way and needed to relearn, or they felt very comfortable and did not wish to have to deal personally with problems such as, for example, deciding as a team how best to allocate workloads. Perhaps they felt this was not their job and they were here to purely execute orders. However, I find that if you accompany people—especially those who are unused to but open to the possibility of change—then the satisfaction, commitment, and impact of employees significantly increase.

Practice, reflect, and adapt—that is the approach I used to train people and change their mindset. We sometimes even started by role playing a different way of working. For example, one aspect is to dare to challenge hierarchies. In a traditional structure, this is often undesired. At the beginning of a meeting, I would assign someone the role of the critical mind. This person's mission was to challenge, ask questions, propose different views and ideas, and never be content with what had been proposed. After a certain time, it became clear how I would react to these types of interactions, and they became more confident that it would be seen as positive to take accountability and to challenge ideas.

Former Middle Managers

One group that has been greatly affected—and to whom change has sometimes been the biggest challenge—are middle managers. The roles of middle managers have been either replaced by a contributor's role (with additional responsibilities but no longer with direct line management) or moved up to a domain leader with a larger remit. Of course, moving "back" to being a single contributor has been the most difficult. This is also when most of the affected people left the organization after a few months. If you want to retain your management, it is crucial to actively involve them in the transformation. They are the ones who may ultimately be the most negatively impacted during the process of transformation.

In particular, as you flatten organizational hierarchies, you will have fewer middle managers. For this group, it will be particularly important to define their new roles and areas of responsibility.

For the ones that stayed, having been away from day-to-day tasks, they felt they had missed the chance to obtain some of these new skills or that they found it difficult to just be part of a team when tasks were allocated instead of what they had previously been used to doing—delegating tasks and managing people. Even if their salary levels were unchanged, most people found that their new roles and responsibilities were not clear, resulting in them feeling undervalued or even demoted in the new organizational setup. What I learnt from this experience was that this middle-management group requires the most attention, and that strong contributors need an even stronger focus to ensure they have an interesting new role and that they feel valued. If they are not leading a team, either on a functional level or online reporting, how can they continue to contribute? How can they accept that this is not a demotion? How do they interact with their team now that they are on the same "flat" level? I realized that in some people's view, we had not given enough attention to this group. I would definitely recommend to focus on key players who are impacted and to define clearly what are delegation "canvas."[3]

---

[3] See http://s3canvas.sociocracy30.org/s3-delegation-canvas.html

Managers of Managers

Managers of managers usually have a lot of different roles in a hierarchical organization. They are responsible for technical (or specific) know-how and line management, for the financial results, for planning and organizing meetings, for information exchange, for moderating at meetings, and for keeping a general track of tasks that need to be carried out by teams. That is quite a lot of things to do—and to balance all at once, as well as representing a great deal of power and decision-making in one pair of hands.

The main challenges for members of this group are to give up some of this power and to share roles within the organization while keeping part of the main responsibility for results. This entails that there need to be lots of trust between leaders and team members. It also means more guidance, vision, strategic thinking, more collaboration, and less top-down decision-making. For the "topic leader," it requires seeking out and leveraging the team's shared know-how rather than taking an "I know best" stance. It is a different story when the leader is an enabler, a sparring partner, a coach, and a challenger who creates an environment that allows the best solutions to be *found* rather than knowing what the best solutions are. It means shifting from control to learning, from decision maker to sparring partner, and from telling to asking. It needs a lot of trust in your team. This is where I invested the most effort and energy, to ensure that team members and their managers would tell me when they faced an issue, identified a risk or encountered a roadblock—so that I could help them solve problems when they needed me.

It might feel like a loss of power for some but with time creates patterns of emulation between leaders and employees. I found that after a period of adjustment many leaders are willing, and most are able, to transform into their new roles. However, this often requires more technical or specialist knowledge than they had previously held (in order to be that sparring partner and not just someone who delegates) and an openness to work as a co-equal with their counterparts, the people (and transformation) managers.

As a leader, I believe you need to *want* to be a servant-oriented leader, to agree to delegate power and decision-making capacity. You will have to prioritize finding the best solution and create the highest impact over your own visibility and ego. That means giving up a "command and control" management style and choosing a "vision, trust, and empower" pathway of leadership.

Even for me it was a transformation that took time. How much do I stay at the "vision" level? How much do I also challenge my team? How deep should I go into a topic and to what extent should I be steering it? I find a valuable way to balance the loss of direct control is by enabling teams to become more transparent. This means sharing what they do and what objectives they would like to put in place for the next quarter. In that way, I could have a chance to ask questions, make suggestions that they might not be aware of, and ensure we are all still aligned. But despite the theory and my committed belief in it, it was also a transformation process for me.

The regular feedbacks we gave each other in the management team is what helped me the most for my own transformation. We were reflecting on how much each of us was living according to our vision and discussing what was needed for us to progress. We would also ask the team on a monthly basis to tell us what we needed to improve, what their challenges were, and how we could help. I also asked my direct reports to immediately tell me, even during a meeting, when they were perceiving me as doing something that was not according to our principles. So I could catch myself, reflect and adapt. I could learn new behaviors for myself. I think it is important to acknowledge that we all have to rewind and this takes practice.

Between a top-down only organization and a bottom-up only, self-organized one, I believe in a model where both views are equally valid and valued.

About Some (Side-)Effects

As I mentioned earlier, the main objective of our transformation was the aim of becoming a more agile organization. Along the way, we realized that besides the benefits we hoped to get, we also had some additional—and mainly positive—effects that were helping us attract talents, creating a more diverse and inclusive environment, or being more resilient and open to change. I would now like to spend some time to share with you how and why we did benefit from this transformative approach.

In our yearly HR review, we saw significant improvement after a year for the following parameters: working with my team, company culture, identification with the company, engagement, and job security. However, the values that related to variables concerning people's feeling of being connected with their teams and superiors were lower. This finding suggests that when people had issues at home, a hard time balancing home and work challenges, they tended to find it more difficult to talk about this with someone from the company.

Attracting talents to IT is a struggle and competition is tough. Employees have a strong lever and their expectations toward employers are multiple. Employees are looking to create a visible impact, having the opportunities to express themselves and be heard, being able to influence and participate in decision-making already at the start of their careers and all the way up. They want to feel they can change things fast and are not bothered by long procedural and administrative processes. They want to be able to make decisions without always requiring higher management to get involved (while the management often have much less expertise in their domain than they themselves). They want, however, to ensure that what they do matters and that their contributions will help them make the next career step. They want to satisfy the customer and anticipate their needs. They are looking for purpose, impact, and a career. The feedback we gathered from our reviews and questionnaires supported the yearly reviews and shows that employee satisfaction increased a year after the start of our transformation, they felt more meaning in their work and felt that more career opportunities were potentially open to them. We were also able to recruit top talents because they were keen to work in this kind of setting and culture.

We also managed to increase diversity in our team in terms of gender, background, language, and origin. What I observed and what people always highlighted in their feedback was that our team was not only diverse but inclusive. I would like to share some remarks about how (I believe) our transformation supported this.

As part of our transformation, we looked closely at how we wanted to structure our meetings, drive discussions, and take decisions. For example, we established processes where, during debates, someone was assigned to moderate and ensure that everyone's voice could be heard. We also often discussed in a "round" format—in other words, someone would present an idea and then, in the first round, everyone would be able to ask as many clarifying questions as they wanted to ensure we all clearly understood the proposition. In the second round, we would take it in turns to share our opinions, give feedback, and challenge the proposition. In this round, there would be no back and forth, where some people would have most of the air time. We would take care that each person had around the same "airtime" and we would also ensure the order in which people spoke would change so that it was not always the same person who would speak first, having more influence. At the end of the round, the person who had proposed the original idea would say how they would take the feedback into account and decide if they wanted to adapt and propose their idea for approval or not. This process would be used equally for all members of a team, independent of their roles, management responsibilities, expertise, or the organizational unit they were working in. We adopted this approach to ensure all views and personalities had an equal voice in how we were discussing and making decisions. By creating rituals, you enable both the more and the less introverted (or extroverted) to participate in and shape the debate. By valuing all viewpoints equally, you can fully leverage all the know-how your team possesses. This does not in itself help to create diversity, but it helps being more inclusive. And because you have an inclusive environment, you become more diverse.

Another advantage of the model is that change is part of the system itself. It is per se resilient. A year and a half after our transformation, the whole IT division would undergo a reorganization. Because we were ahead of the change and our people already had more experience, they were more open to and positive about its potential upsides. They found it easy to adapt.

I could, however, see some risks in this model that could affect people's resilience. The fact that people work on different projects and work issues with different teams may weaken the bonds between and within some teams. And that in turn can lead to some staff members feeling less attached to a team. They might be less likely to spontaneously offer support to others, forcing a cultural shift where it becomes each individual's responsibility to ask their peers for help when they need it.

About Driving an Organization: A Top-Down or Bottom-Up Transformation

In a hierarchical organization, it is clear that decisions are taken top-down.

Pure top-down gives clarity. It is about following orders. You do what you are told and when something unexpected, unclear, or conflicting happens, you can delegate upward to resolve issues. It makes employees' lives rather simple, and their objective is to do the tasks requested of them. It has value in ensuring the organization is driven and aligned by top decision-makers. It relies on top managers having broad and deep knowledge that allows them to make decisions that impact all areas of the company. It gives coherence across the decisions and makes it easier for an organization to understand and follow a clear direction. You will be measured on how successful you have been at doing what you were told. Typical measures are percentage of delivery on time, on budget, and on scope (whether this relates to a project, a program, or other tasks). You have objectives that describe out*put* rather than out*come*.

The challenge today is that we live in a VUCA (volatile, unpredictable, complex, ambiguous) world. No top manager can master all the required expertise on their own. Decision-making is not about taking *the* right decision as a one-time event but is often more about an iterative process where you adapt and fine-tune next steps toward a vision or a north star.

Those decisions are smaller and often better made by experts than by generalist managers. It allows you to leverage the expertise of the whole organization, to adapt, to get buy-in. But this calls for greater maturity, autonomy, and accountability from each employee. You ask them not only that they understand the task they need to complete but that they understand what you are trying to achieve, what are the expected impacts, and ask them to define the way to achieve it. They will need to spend more time thinking about what they do, how they do it, and why. It makes them accountable for the decisions they have taken and to resolve more issues among themselves before escalating upward.

The risks of having a purely top-down organization (in particular for larger organizations) lie in a possible lack of adaptability, the danger that decisions are made by non-experts, a lower commitment of the employee toward vision and outcome, the downsides of a purely bottom-up organization (or self-organization) lie in a lack of coherence, redundancies, a lower propensity for risk-taking and a lesser likelihood that bold and visionary decision-making occurs.

When we started our transformation, the discussions around what is the right balance of top-down and bottom-up steering have been intensive. It started with how and who would participate in defining and driving our transformation. On one hand, I believed it was important to give a clear vision of the "why"—that is, of the purpose of the transformation and what we wanted to achieve. For this, I was in the leading role and took first my management team onboard to challenge and further define our vision. On the other hand, it was important to set a signal from the beginning that the role and expectations toward employees were changing and that I wanted and needed them to participate, take ownership, and be accountable for the outcome our team was delivering.

For this to succeed, I did not want to wait for the "go live" phase of our new operating model, but wanted to start immediately. I wanted the process to be more than a "project" but already the start of our transformation. This is why we did not do a project with a project manager executing decisions for the sponsor and steering committee. In addition, we wanted the process to be a transformation with no beginning and end. After showing the team why we needed to transform and sharing some of the ideas we had, we shared all our documents. I mean all, including our draft documents. Anyone was free to use them, give feedback, write comments, and share ideas. Even if it had an impact on people, their position, and their roles and responsibilities, we wanted to lead by example. So, we created a culture of transparency.

We also tried to involve as many people as possible. Every person that was interested to shape and define our new ways of working was welcomed. We created "thinktanks" responsible to further defining different topics (for example, relating to role definition, communications, service manuals, catalogs, and introduction packs for new staff). These thinktanks then evolved, with some people taking on more leads and others fewer. We held sessions where the thinktank members and management would sit down together and exchange updates on progress with each other. It is crucial that these discussions were designed to take place "on the same level." Some management staff made themselves available to the thinktank teams as a sparring partner to help align our thoughts. We also made sure that management representatives would present their progress and ideas to the thinktank teams for their review and approval. In this way, the communication and discussions happened in a natural and organic fashion. We, of course, also held "all-in" sessions more to formalize the information and ensure no one would feel left out.

Changing from the inside can be more difficult and slower but, when you achieve it, it is more lasting.

We also received invaluable support from an external coach and from our HR specialist. They played, in my view, a key role because they were familiar with our culture and processes. They were a neutral person and could help us identify any potential sources of conflict or resistance, lack of communication and were eager to see us succeed. I would strongly recommend having one or two such people when you want to transform an organization.

What is interesting is that we got most of the resistance from the people that were not part of our unit and usually with those who interacted with us least. It seems to me that the transformation we had started challenged many. Added to less understanding of what we were doing and what we hoped to achieve, it took a long time to convince our colleagues. I admit that I underestimated this part and if I would do it again, I would spend more time communicating to and managing buy-in from stakeholders. After more than a year, we managed to demonstrate the value of what we were doing to more people, and this was mainly accomplished by my team. They were spreading the word about what we were doing and the benefits they experienced first hand. Sharing the idea with their friends and colleagues created a "movement" internally and helped to get sufficient support to scale our transformation to the whole IT department and even some other business units.

3   Change Outcome: Success, Yes or No? How Did the Change Participants Measure the Outcome?

Measuring the Progress and Success of the Transformation

At the beginning of our transformation, we set out goals and objectives as to why we wanted to transform and what we wanted to achieve. We wanted to measure our progress and to be able to learn, support, and adapt. This was more internally focused on how well we did according to our plan, whether the transformation team was on track and genuinely living the new habits, how it was being perceived and whether people were happy and feeling the positive effects of this change.

We took different actions to ensure this was done:

1. An agile transformation expert, who attended all the team meetings. He helped the team to create new habits, use new tools in their day-to-day lives. The expert was not there to give training or teach theoretical principles but much more to identify when old habits would kick in and help create new ones, practicing with participants how to do it. This was the occasion to gather challenges, questions, deal with skepticism, and to get a general feel for the progress the teams were making.

2. The weeks before and after the changes, we also offered call-in sessions, where anyone would be free to join, ask questions to me, experts, or each other. The transformation team would hereby gain a sense of what was still unclear and be able to feel what support, clarification, or adjustment were needed.

3. We held an "opinion leader" meeting each month. These leaders were chosen by the team to represent their idea, share the state of the transformation, participate in shaping changes, and to communicate how the team felt.

4. On a monthly basis, I would review the list of employees with the agile transformation expert, as well as with the Head of People and Performance and we would ask ourselves who was at risk of leaving,

not supporting the transformation, what were the main blockers and how we could support them.

5. We also had anonymized questionnaires to team members on top of the yearly employee satisfaction review done for the whole company.

Those were some indicators that helped us support the team, in particular during the first months of our transformation and to adjust course.

On the other side, while looking at our team, processes and employee satisfaction in a more introspective way, we also looked at external feedback. What we compared is peer perception and satisfaction. Were the objectives we set were achieved? We also measured employee satisfaction and overall performance, as well as OKR delivery.

We planned retrospective and learning sessions which included our partner, colleagues from other units, and our team. We adapted many of our processes and even roles, and will continue to do so.

Overall, I am convinced our transformation effort was very successful even though we faced strong skepticism at the beginning, when many doubted whether we would deliver results and generate value for the whole organization. From our yearly employee survey to the impact measure through OKR to the feedback from our colleagues and partners on the diverse, resilient, attractive, and customer-oriented culture we created, all show positive progress after a year. And there is no better proof to me when I see that most elements of our transformation have now been scaled to the whole IT division and to some other business units. I believe we were successful—not because everything went perfectly from day one—but because we listened to each other's concerns and made many adaptations along the way (for example, relating to the number of roles, the number of roles a person should take, communication outside our team, and other variables). We also ensured that teams could enjoy some flexibility when it came to how they were adopting the tools (avoiding "one size fits all" approaches and being careful not to over-define). The main challenge is to find the right balance between managing an organization top-down and bottom-up.

4   A Final Retrospective on the Change Process: Pros and Cons, Recommendations and Action Plan for Stakeholders, Lessons Learnt, Surprising Successes

I started the transformation of my team into a rather traditional, hierarchical, and large organization. This presented its own challenges, and it took time to convince people of the worth of the transformational approach. I took this approach to just try and not to ask for "permission." It was risky, and I had to spend extra time afterward. But I am not sure I would have been able to do it otherwise. The great part is that I can witness how much impact a model like this can have, and the improvements were visible and significant.

It amazed me to see how many people got interested and chose to try splitting functional and line reporting. While many thought it would be difficult to recruit for the role of people manager in an IT organization, this turned out not to be the case. In fact, these positions were the ones that attracted the most candidates.

Consent-based decision-making was another tool that many adapted, and we got a lot of positive feedback. Even if it requires discipline and a lot of practice, the discussions and decisions are so much more streamlined and still with a high buy-in. OKRs or the "canvas" tool (to define a domain and its purpose) have also been used by many teams which surprised me as these methods were sometimes adopted by those who had initially criticized the sociocracy model.

Overall, I would recommend everyone to at least be curious and look at this model of organizational transformation more closely. I would not advise people to just follow everything but to look at the pain points you are trying to solve and see which pattern, template, or tool could be most useful for your organization.

If you are considering more extensive changes, while I see many benefits to this model, I would warn against some pitfalls. For example, people need to belong and to be part of a team. This need—and the feeling that you have a close circle of colleagues who have your back and care, especially for you, is something that is less present in this model. So, I would really look at strategies that address this deficiency. I would also recommend keeping the number of roles to a minimum, maintaining at least some degree of stability in how roles are assigned and communicated, and avoid having people work in more than two domains. Make things as simple as possible.

For a team or a company to remain competitive and attract talent (younger generations), to be more agile and to have a committed, value-driven, and customer-oriented workforce, I believe management needs to look at new operating models like the one we tried and find which elements could be integrated.

Appendix

Role	Definition
Circle Lead	Assumes the meaning/goal/purpose of the circles and is responsible for achieving the circle's goals
Economist	Responsible for maintaining transparency when it comes to budgets, efficiency, and impacts
Coordinator	Responsible for moderating efficient and effective meetings
Secretary	Assists in the conducting of meetings; plans and documents decisions
Representative General Circle	Assumes the meaning/goal/purpose of the circle and represents the interest of the circle to the general circle
Representative Peer Circle	Represents to the peer circle the interest of the circle they belong to
Expert	Responsible for the tasks assigned to them in their area of work (e.g., enterprise architect, quality manager, and process manager)

References

Bernstein, E., Bunch, J., & Canner, N., & Lee, M. (2016). Beyond the holacracy hype. *Harvard Business Review*. Retrieved January 21, 2023, from https://hbr.org/2016/07/beyond-the-holacracy-hype

Block, C. (2002). 12 reasons your digital transformation will fail. *Forbes*. Retrieved December 20, 2022, from https://www.forbes.com/sites/forbescoa chescouncil/2022/03/16/12-reasons-your-digital-transformation-will-fail/?sh=24fd445d1f1e

Laetitia Henriot Arsever is a passionate advocate of customer-centric digitalization, driving innovation and transformation at the intersection of IT and business. She is an authentic leader engaged in developing people and challenging the status quo. As a strong believer in AI, Cloud, IoT and Blockchain as long-term game changers, she leverages technology to create value with and for people.

Laetitia is currently Head of IT and Digital (CDIO) at Valora. She holds a Master degree in Computer Science from the EPFL (École Polytechnique Fédérale Lausanne), Switzerland. Before joining Valora in November 2022, she was a member of the executive board of IT at Swiss Post, heading the department of Technology, Strategy and Steering. Before that, she was CIO EMEA at the elevator company Schindler, where she worked in various positions for over 10 years. She set up Schindler's digital innovation hub in Berlin and held positions in finance, sales, and operations, which gave her a broad and strategic perspective. Before that, she was an analyst and full-stack developer at the consulting firm BearingPoint Switzerland for 2 years.

Pivoting to a Web3 Product and Building a Healthy Remote Culture with Human-Centric Leadership

Felicia Würtenberger

1 Introduction

Flooz Inc. is a Web3 startup with a crypto wallet, trading platform, and infrastructure product offering. Flooz's vision is to humanize the Web3 and crypto space by focusing on an intuitive user experience and abstracting complex technological concepts to onboard the next 100 million people onto the blockchain. The 25 team members at Flooz operate fully remotely from more than 12 countries and four different time zones. Global lockdowns at that time were one of the main drivers to founding a fully remote company. This was beneficial to attract the right talent and to stay flexible with constantly changing external conditions.

Before we continue, let us understand Web 3.0 and the difference between Web 1.0 and Web 2.0:

F. Würtenberger (✉)
Flooz Inc., West-Hollywood, CA, USA

91

Subject	Description	Company examples
Web 1.0	Web 1.0 was the first stage of the world wide web evolution. The core purpose for the user was " read-only" because of its static content. The economy that was shaped during this time was the *information economy* offering basic encyclopedias.	Google, Internet Explorer, MSN
Web 2.0	The evolution of Web 2.0 brought social interactions between users, dynamic user-generated content, and the ability to create communities on social media platforms. This also introduced monetizing user data and the rise of targeted marketing campaigns. The *platform economy* is a fundamental part of Web 2.0.	Facebook, Snapchat, TikTok, Amazon, YouTube, Uber
Web 3.0 (Web3)	Web 3.0 is the next evolution of the world wide web. It is based on the blockchain and is a decentralized online ecosystem. It is a direct content-to-user connection without intermediaries who are controlling or owning content, data, and assets. As a user, you own every asset, all data, and every piece of content you created. This new web technology evolution initiated the *ownership economy*.	Ethereum, Binance, Consensys (MetaMask), Brave, OpenSea, Dapper

Source: Own illustration

This vision was different when Flooz was founded in early 2021 during the COVID-19 pandemic. The initial business journey started in Web 2.0, with a link-in-bio tool offering targeting creators and influencers to empower them in monetizing their follower base. An unforeseeable event during the first year of the company's existence—a successful innovation sprint that launched a crypto token—led to a strategic pivot that initiated change on all levels of the company.

What exactly happened? Some of the Flooz team members were very interested in the Web3 space and had been experimenting with blockchain-based products. The first thing that they wanted to learn was writing a smart contract on the blockchain, which became the subject of the innovation sprint. The result coming out of this experiment was a crypto token based on the Ethereum Blockchain. After the first days of launch, the token gained much traction. People started investing, and a few weeks later, we had a community of nearly 10,000 token holders.

We quickly realized that investing in a crypto token is not as easy as making a bank transfer or buying something online. The digital products and services out there, like trading platforms or crypto wallets, are far from user-friendly and require a lot of research and education before a user feels confident enough to use them. Experiencing this first-hand after launching the token, we had a strong conviction that mass adoption in the Web3 and blockchain space will be driven by user-friendly interfaces and intuitive digital products.

After assessing the core capabilities of the team (building consumer-facing products) and the market opportunity (little competition in an uprising multi-billion dollar industry), Flooz decided to fully commit to Web3 at the beginning of 2022. The new mission to humanize crypto was born, and the team had to shift their previous focus entirely onto building new products for a different target audience.

Our new digital product offering includes a decentralized crypto trading platform and a multi-chain crypto wallet. The trading platform has been assigned to our cross-functional web development team, which has previously been working on our web creator platform. Our cross-functional mobile development team, which has been working on our creator tool app, switched to developing our mobile wallet.

This strategic shift and change affected the young organization on all levels. We had to reshuffle the teams according to the new requirements. Our engineering team had to learn several new technologies (e.g., solidity code for smart contracts) and get familiar with different blockchains (e.g., Ethereum, Binance Smart Chain, and Polygon). Our product team had to go back to zero and start doing fundamental product research about crypto trading platforms and wallets. New business and security concepts had to emerge. And marketing, growth, and partnerships had to start getting familiar with our new customers and target audience.

Zooming in, we still had to build fundamental organizational structures, cultural rituals, and processes for a 1-year-old company. Besides business success and offering desirable Web3 products, Flooz's goal is to build a strong and healthy remote organization to navigate the ups and downs in an early-stage environment. One of the biggest challenges of remote startups like Flooz is to build a healthy and vivid culture that nourishes connections and makes people feel they belong and are their best selves at work.

The senior management of Flooz decided early on that this pivotal change needs to be carefully guided and implemented to align with our organizational goal of ensuring employees' emotional and mental well-being. Therefore, we are committed to giving a clear direction, providing transparency, involving team members, and leading with empathy and emotional intelligence. Looking at change leadership literature, this strong human-centered approach deviates "from linear, technocratic and hierarchical models of leadership and change toward cultivating engagement, connection, and collaboration" (O'Brien, 2022, p. 20).

Our leadership principles are heavily inspired by the approach of vulnerable and servant leadership, which has been rising for the past decade. Thought leaders like Bréne Brown, who spoke about "The power of vulnerability" during her TED talk in 2010, and Claude Silver, who has been Chief Heart Officer at VaynerMedia since 2014, are pioneering a human way of leading businesses through their life cycles of growth and change. Concepts of emotional optimism and positive language are also mentioned by Silver. Back in the nineties, Daniel Goleman, a US psychologist, and science author, already discovered that boosting collective emotional intelligence is one of the main drivers of thriving high-performing teams (Goleman, 1996, p. 163), especially in the knowledge-worker industries.

This chapter will showcase Flooz's human-centered approach to the extensive change processes leading to pivoting into a new industry.

2 Pitfalls and Learnings

Looking at the challenges, pitfalls, and learnings, it is essential to mention that driving organizational growth and shifting strategic direction in a remote setup was a new challenge for everyone at Flooz. At the same time, considering Flooz had been around just a few months, nobody expected to be working on a new product and problem space soon. The management team at Flooz had decided to pivot into Web3 without prior experience in this space and was looking into a future full of uncertainties. Past change management and leadership experiences were based on working on-site and relying on physical presence. We were all aware of this in the management team and agreed on an optimistic mindset, positive language, and an experimental approach to cultivate change within Flooz.

Reading about change management theories and models, you often encounter a very linear approach that seems to offer structure and predictability. This predictability comes from a static process including separate stages and control mechanisms. The downside of following this approach is that it dehumanizes organizations as it rules out any space for creativity, flexibility, or experimentation (O'Brien, 2022, p. 29).

Fritzenschaft (2014)identified critical success factors of change management in empirical research. A strongly defined vision, full commitment, and support from the management team were the top-rated factors in initiating change on a strategic management level. The most critical success factors at a team member level are creating a shared problem awareness and transparent communication of upcoming changes (Fritzenschaft, 2014, p. 64). The human component has already been more present in Fritzenschaft's research and findings.

How did we at Flooz experience the change process? What were the learnings, what worked well, and where did we encounter challenges or failed?

As mentioned in the introduction, pivoting into a new industry does not mean a mere change for a specific team or process. It affects the whole organization on all levels. Let us take a look at our product, people, and remote culture through the lens of being a human-centered company.

2.1   Product

On a product level, we encountered along the way that we were trying to solve too many challenges at the same time. This led to a burn of resources, time, and budget on projects that were not entirely thought through or not prioritized well enough to be aligned with the overall goal. This led to frustration, confusion, and misalignment across the product and tech teams.

This particular situation could be considered a pitfall, as it brought some of our employees to the verge of burnout and hurt us financially as a young startup. Being a company that puts people and their well-being at the center, we realized that we are violating our values and what we stand for. Our team leads and other team members have also proactively addressed this.

As mentioned, change is not a static and linear process where you have a 5-step plan, and once you finish, you have the desired result. The pivot into Web3 looked messy and chaotic in this particular part of our organization. The management team did not have all the answers, so we did a few things that helped us to create more clarity, alignment, and balance inside the product teams:

- We learned that we needed to be clearer about our vision and break it down into actionable goals.
- We agreed to challenge each other more and invest more time in enforcing organizational alignment.
- We realized that we needed one product roadmap for our crypto wallet and one for our trading platform, planning for at least 10–12 weeks. This ensured stability and focus for everyone building our core products.
- We listened to the frustrations of our team members and defined boundaries (e.g., turning off notifications after working hours), processes (e.g., design reviews), and other action items (e.g., regular check-ins on mental and emotional well-being).
- We organized learning sessions across the organization to learn about "Web3 basics," "Security in DeFi," and other more technical deep dives. This fostered collective learning as everyone was new to this domain and was a driver of trust and ownership across the team.

2.2   People

According to Google's internal research study, psychological safety is one of the main ingredients that makes up a high-performing team (ReWork,

2022). Looking at the people at Flooz and how they experienced the change, one of our key learnings was that we had to bring emotions and feelings to the surface.

The feelings we noticed coming up during the challenges described earlier were frustration, grief, doubt, surprise, and joy. Every human has feelings that occur when needs are not being met, difficult memories are triggered, or achievements are not being seen and appreciated. Dan Cable, a professor of organizational behavior in London, states that ensuring employees' self-expression leads to more creativity and fosters trust (2019, p. 60).

Our main learning was to realize that we must share and process people's emotions in a very open, collective, and authentic way to foster psychological safety, proactiveness, and self-organization within the team. This was our antidote to what people often struggle with in a remote setup: feeling isolated, lack of motivation due to poor communication, and unclear direction. We created rituals that nurtured this way of speaking from everyone's heart and made sure to process worries, doubts, or fears and celebrate personal events like getting married or moving into a new apartment.

Every week we start with our Monday Mug session, which is exactly designed for what was described above: creating psychological safety in a remote setup.

Monday Mug Session

Purpose: Having a mindful and collective start to the week as a remote team, sharing personal experiences and holding space for each other.

Ceremony Procedure: Everyone dials in with a cup of coffee/tea, and team members share their experiences from the weekend. The latest developments in the world or the industry are often discussed. We try to make this session not about work or the company but about the people themselves and what they are currently experiencing in their lives.

Duration: Weekly on Mondays/60 mins.

Participants: Internal team.

Ceremony Moderator: Ideally, someone from the senior management team or the founder, as it emphasizes that the company's leadership cares about people and reassures people to show up for each other continuously.

Amplifying culture: This session creates belonging and connection throughout the entire organization as you are getting to know a person over time. You learn about each other's favorite things to do, or you know when someone has an important moment in their life happening or coming up (e.g., a wedding, the birth of a child, vacation, and travels). You laugh with each other, and you hold space for each other, which is a natural and authentic way of building a relationship despite the remote working environment. This session creates a recurring rhythm that team members can rely on, especially during times of change.

2.3   Remote Culture

From the beginning, we knew that the culture we wanted to build is people centered and empowering to become a (remote) place that our employees truly enjoy. As mentioned, we actively invested in this approach by becoming aware of our shortcomings as a leadership team and the conscious decision to lead in a compassionate and vulnerable way. To put our culture at the forefront of our company during the change process, we established an organizational vision similar to the product vision and roadmap we created.

From this vision, we derived strategic missions to ensure that we are not losing track during the journey of our full pivot. Part of these missions were recurring ceremonies and rituals (e.g., our Monday Mug) that supported us in finding ways to lead by example, create a clear focus, and guide the whole organization through the strategic shift. The missions also contributed (and still do) to building a strong cultural foundation that aims at our organizational goal of being people-centric and putting employees' well-being first.

A challenge that we did not overcome was having people on the team working from the USA or Asia. Especially during a change project, you need to have frequent check-ins and meetings to ensure everyone is on board and on track. Having more than 6 h of time difference within a team did not work for us. We learned that an operating time zone of

CET ± 3 h works best for us in terms of having a few hours overlap for initiatives and ceremonies that are crucial for culture building and change management as an early-stage business.

3   Change Outcome

The outcome can be considered successful by looking at the company's current state and reflecting on the past months. We have established a strong change culture and launched the newly developed crypto products within the period that we aimed for. The next step is to scale our user base and organization to establish traction and foster business growth.

On a product level, we have a much more solid foundation and are in a more stable place than before. Our product managers learned to say "no" and stick to the roadmap and prioritization. We have filled the knowledge gaps and built up Web3 and blockchain expertise to a point where our people are becoming subject matter experts to the outside. We underestimated that not everyone is passionate about the industry we entered, leading to people not caring as much about the products they build as they used to do. Going forward, this topic needs to be addressed, as it will have a long-term effect on motivation and emotional well-being.

Looking at our team at Flooz, we have created a safe space and made people feel belong. During the change process, we had to part ways with some of our team members for different reasons, but the most unexpected was that being in the USA did not work for us from a time zone perspective. We also learned that mental health is even more under attack in Web3. The crypto industry never sleeps. It is a buzzing space 24/7, which makes it hard for people to go offline and have a regular work week. We had to actively prevent people from working the whole weekend and supported those who had anxiety attacks because of the instability of the markets. We were unaware of this before entering Web3 and were concerned about the potential negative effects of this industry on our team members.

Implementing recurring alignment meetings and ceremonies at Flooz with senior management involvement led to amplifying and anchoring the new mission and problem space throughout the organization at

Flooz. We also involved employees early on in our planning and preparation for change. For example, after announcing the decision to do a complete pivot, we involved all team members in shaping this change by researching and coming up with solutions and ideas for their domain. Following a collective change approach, our team members felt safe experimenting and did not have the feeling that they were alone in the unknown.

We asked our team members how they feel working at Flooz after the change, and they replied:

- At Flooz, you are free as an individual but pushing limits as a team.
- The company culture at Flooz allows you to be free and choose your tasks.
- You can easily be yourself at Flooz and be open about your needs. It feels very human to work at Flooz.

In the end, we managed the business and product pivot successfully. Additionally, we created a fertile environment to nourish people driven by curiosity and a growth mindset. This will help to navigate future pivots and changes more easily, as change is inherent to a company's DNA, and you need people who embrace uncertainty and love to solve challenges.

4   Final Retrospective

Looking back at the past year, Flooz has been going through constant change and adaptation. Summarizing our lessons learned and reflecting on our routines established doubles down for us on vulnerable leadership and creating spaces of authentic, honest, and connecting experiences.

Regular reflection and check-ins as a team are beneficial to achieving mental and emotional well-being across the organization. It helps to digest the uncertainty that comes with change, processes emotions, and supports visualizing progress and personal growth. Especially in times when people are losing track or seeing others getting frustrated with what they are doing.

A company culture that promotes authenticity, vulnerability, and the commitment to achieve a common goal that serves a greater purpose while turning everything towards a new direction is based on trust and resilience. We could only accomplish this by choosing a people-first and humanistic leadership approach from the beginning.

To root this approach into our culture and organizational mindset early on, we established ceremonies and rituals that helped drive our approach's activation and adoption.

Change Management Checklist (in a fully remote setup):

- Create virtual rituals and ceremonies that become cultural artifacts, connecting people, and giving them a recurring structure.
- Ensure that people feel impactful and strongly connected to the company's vision and purpose.
- Change is never favorable for a human being. Our mind is programmed to keep things under control to survive. Go the extra mile, be close to your people, and ask how they feel about changes or decisions being made. Bring feelings to the surface.
- Double down on psychological safety, lead with compassion, and make people feel seen and heard in the organization.
- Offer mentoring to people and establish regular knowledge exchange. This accelerates change.
- Break the silence for the team, especially in a Zoom call. Admitting that you do not have all the answers promotes trust and makes people comfortable speaking up and engaging.
- Facilitate meetings, ceremonies, and cultural rituals in a way that always supports absorbing information and processing emotions.
- Focus on positive language, as language is essential during pivots and change. People tend to get uncomfortable and see challenges, focusing on solutions and opportunities.
- Make handling change a collaborative learning effort so no one feels like the "stupid" person in the room.

As a final thought, adaptation is key when implementing approaches to drive change and create a culture around this. Ultimately, the strategy, rituals, and ceremonies you choose depend highly on the company's DNA and the future state that the change project is aiming for.

References

Cable, D. (2019). *Alive at work*. Harvard Business Review Press.
Fritzenschaft, T. (2014). *Critical success factors of change management: An empirical research in German small and medium-sized enterprises*. Springer Gabler.
Goleman, D. (1996). *Emotional intelligence*. Bloomsbury.
O'Brien, M. (2022). *The new leaders of change*. PCL.
ReWork Project Aristotles. (2022). *Guide: Understand team effectiveness*. Retrieved October 30, 2022, from https://rework.withgoogle.com/print/guides/5721312655835136

Felicia Würtenberger is the Chief Human Resources Officer at Flooz Inc. Her academic background is in business and organizational psychology. During her professional career, she has been mostly part of early and later-stage startups in the digital economy sector (e.g., Kitchen Stories, Klarna, and kollex).

She has been part of Flooz since its early beginnings and built up the remote culture from day one in close sparring and collaboration with the founder and senior management of the company. Her core tasks include defining the organizational roadmap, driving strategic missions and growth, and implementing the cultural pillars across the organization.

While building the foundations of a remote company and a healthy organizational culture, Flooz strategically pivoted from the creator economy into the Web3 economy. Looking at this pivot as a change project, Felicia's role was to prepare the organization to digest, plan and execute this change successfully.

Community Building in Change Processes

Sara Noronha Ramos

1 Introduction

The project hereby described was created within the Learning Day Community, a digital space where mindful lifelong learners work on personal growth together.

The change proposed by Learning Day focuses on both the societal and the individual levels. It is the transformation from seeing learning as contained in the classroom to something that happens every day; from happening when we were kids to happening every day until we die; from being a burden to being a source of a joyful and meaningful life.

> The technological, demographic and global changes have exacerbated the need to reframe learning with a lifelong perspective.—OECD Skills Outlook 2021: Learning for Life

S. N. Ramos (✉)
Learning Day, Porto, Portugal
e-mail: hello@learningday.community

As a business leader, I am sure you recognize the need to constantly adapt in your day-to-day and how hard it can be to carve time to learn new skills or even stay up to date with the non-stop influx of information and demands coming your way. How might we balance these two seemingly opposed views?

As an individual, the evident impacts of the climate crisis, the rapid technological change and digitalization, and the sudden shocks like the COVID-19 pandemic, among others, require you to change your behaviors and mindset, while trying to do your best to meet the increasing demands of life.

> The burdens of life have never been heavier.—Esther Perel

This is the context in which the Weekly Reflection Sessions (WRS) came to life.

> In a fast-changing and uncertain world, lifelong learning can help individuals adapt and become resilient to external shocks, lowering their vulnerability.—OECD Skills Outlook 2021: Learning for Life

WRS started as an experiment inspired by Kolb's Experiential Learning Theory (Kolb, 1984) (Fig. 1).

Learning from experiences

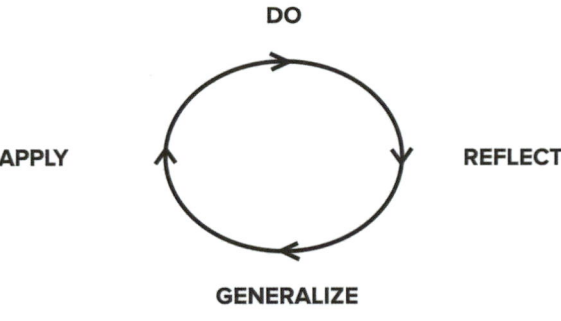

Experiential Learning Theory (Kolb,1984)

Fig. 1 Experiential learning theory. Source: Own illustration based on Kolb (1984)

Experiential Learning is the process of learning new skills, knowledge, behaviors, and attitudes through active reflection after the experience itself.

Kolb's (1984) Experiential Learning Theory presents a cycle of four elements:

1. Concrete Experience (DO)
2. Reflective Observation (REFLECT)
3. Abstract Conceptualization (GENERALIZE)
4. Active Experimentation (APPLY)

The cycle begins with an experience that the individual has had, followed by an opportunity to reflect on that experience. After that, the person is invited to conceptualize and draw conclusions about what they experienced and observed, leading to future actions in which they apply what they learned and experiment with different behaviors, and the cycle continues.

When I observed this model, I realized that we spend all of our waking time "doing" things, but we are missing the crucial step to turn those experiences into learning opportunities: reflection. I saw how we are wasting learning potential in our days.

The invitation was simple: join me on Zoom to reflect individually and then, if you want, share your reflections in a small group. That was it! 26 people joined the first session, participants kept returning week after week and the feedback was overwhelmingly positive. I knew I was on to something.

> I was more conscious of my actions which is exactly what I was hoping to get out of reflections. I want to live my life with more intent and reflecting on what happened definitely helps with that a lot.—participant

> The sessions are creating space for me to think more deeply. I looked back at my week 1 challenges and got some real insight about how things had moved on.—participant

Before I demonstrate why this can be useful to you in a change management context, allow me to explain exactly what happens in the Weekly Reflection Sessions.

The process was designed with the following principles in mind:

- Everyone is invited.
- Not sharing is OK. Sharing is also fine.
- No commitment to return or show up every week.
- Every day is a learning day.

These principles are translated into a format in two parts:

- Part 1–20 min of individual reflection.
- Part 2–20 min of facilitated group sharing (optional).

When the participants join the online session, they hear instrumental-only music and see a slide on the screen with a reflection prompt that is designed to get them going through the learning cycle as defined by Kolb (1984) and described above.

- What happened this week? >> Recall experience/DO.
- (Example question; this changes every week) What have I prioritized? >> Focus/REFLECT.
- What have I learned about myself, others, or the world? >> Insight/GENERALIZE.
- How am I going to incorporate what I learned in the rest of the week? >> Action/APPLY (Fig. 2).

The second part of the session is optional and has two rules of engagement:

- If you are sharing, speak from the "I"—you are the expert of your experience.
- If you are listening, hold space for others (Fig. 3).

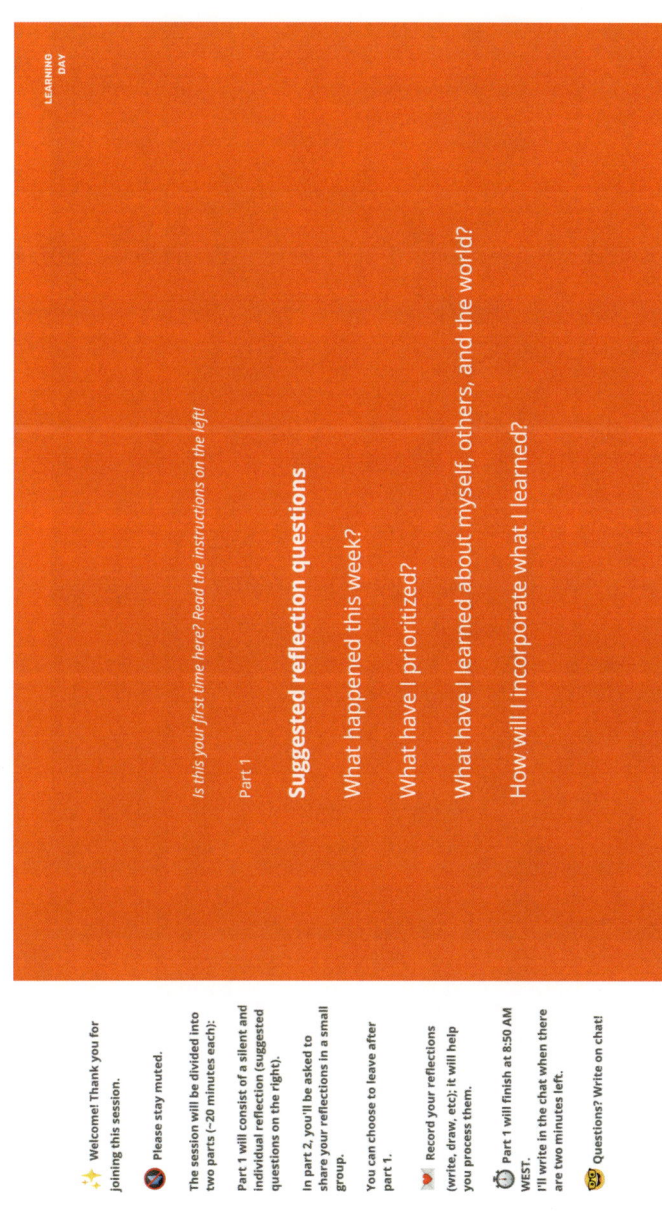

Fig. 2 Typical instructions for a weekly reflection session. Source: Own illustration

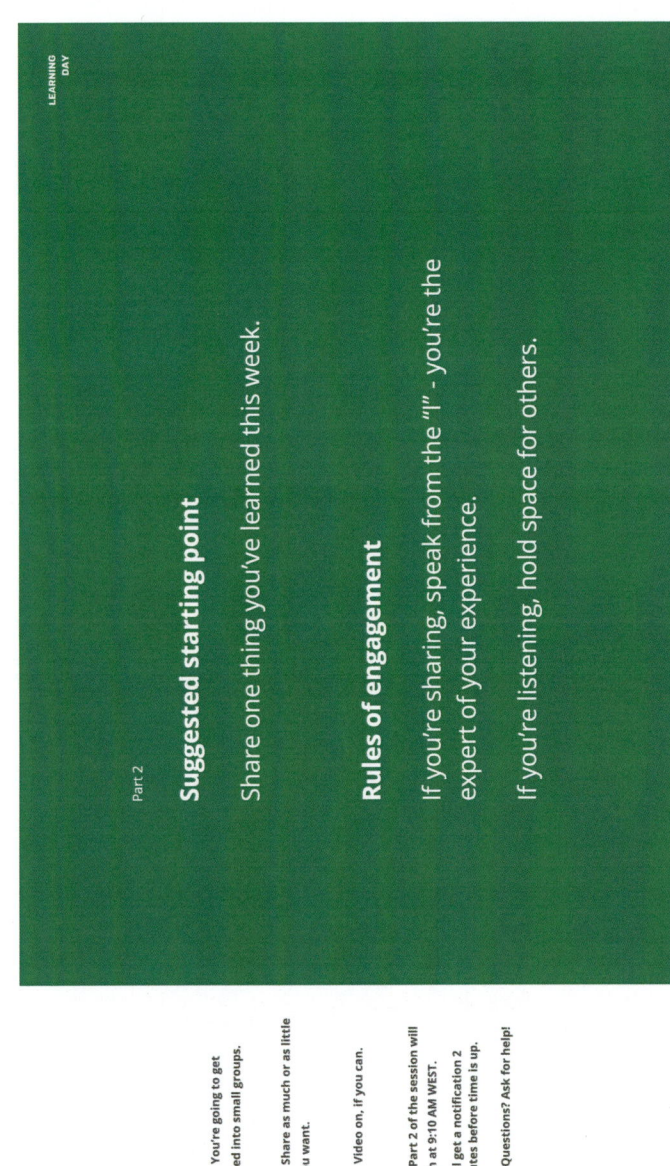

Fig. 3 Typical instructions for a weekly reflection session. Source: Own illustration

These ground rules intend to remind the participants that their experience is valid and welcome (you are the expert of your experience) but that it should not be generalized (speak from the "I"), and that they should actively listen and allow others to express themselves freely, without judgment.

The sharing starts with an invitation for each participant to share one thing they learned that week and then the facilitator can open the conversation for more reflections and comments.

Now that you know how the process unfolds, in the following section, I will share how this can be useful in change management context and surface learnings and pitfalls identified by me as the host of open reflection sessions and by two organizations who have either tried to or successfully implemented this process—Municipality Org (Sweden) and RnDAO (remote-only). In both cases, the process was brought to the organizations through individuals in leadership positions who joined the Weekly Reflection Sessions hosted by the Learning Day Community.

In Municipality Org's case, the intention was to support one of their teams to fully adopt and integrate three guiding principles—anti-discrimination, equality, and gender equality. After doing baseline work to understand to what extent they were or were not working according to the principles, the leadership identified the need to encourage team members to take time to think about and reflect on these principles and how to apply them.

RnDAO is an innovative DAO (Decentralized Autonomous Organization), with a mission to empower humane collaboration and enable a humane vision of Web3 and all the new digital products emerging in this space.

They brought the WRS process into the organization to pave the way toward being a "high-functioning learning organism," starting at the onboarding of new collaborators.

When I started asking folks who had been "onboarded" what they learned last week, it became clear that there was not enough space for this reflection. We often get caught up in doing without taking the time to reflect on what we are learning and how we can incorporate those learnings into what we do next.

By creating an intentionally facilitated space for this reflection the hope is that we build muscles individually and then within the community to track, reflect on and share our learnings so that we and others can build on top of what we know now.—Ray Kanani, RnDAO

2   Learnings and Pitfalls

My biggest learning is simple: the human experience is universal, even if we go through it in different contexts and realities. We are a lot more similar than we are different. In times of deep fracture in our societies, of decreasing mental health and increasing loneliness, this learning might be the most important of all.

Reflection might be an individual process, but when shared with others, in a safe space, we are flexing our empathy and compassion muscles, toward others and ourselves, we are allowing others to keep us accountable and to realize the progress and change we do not see in ourselves.

The Weekly Reflection Sessions became a reliable space for many people. The consistency of the process brings them comfort, even when they are asked to confront their emotions and difficult experiences. On the other hand, the novelty introduced by the reflection prompts that change every week opens up unexpected connections and insights.

I have also found that my active participation, or of anyone else facilitating the sessions, is essential to set the tone and the example. If I am asking the community to be honest and vulnerable, I need to be the first to do it. This makes the full presence of the facilitator critical to the success of the process. For this reason, I recommend that you have more than one facilitator for this initiative, to make sure that at least one person is available, time and emotionally wise, to be present. Additionally, this also ensures the initiative is not dependent on anyone, in case one of the facilitators leaves the organization, as it happened in Municipality Org's case.

In the context of the development and launch of digital products, this process—and reflection and community, more broadly—can become the anchor, the stable ground, to cope with the turmoil. As I started a new role at Management 3.0 in 2021 to design and build their private online community, the Weekly Reflection Sessions became a space to process the uncertainty, the doubt, the setbacks, and the victories.

For those following or implementing agile methodologies in their digital product development and/or change management initiatives, the parallels seem obvious to me. Reflection supports the experimentation mindset and the regular retrospective moments between development cycles, and community building might be an essential key ingredient for high-performing cross-functional teams.

> An organizational memo and slide deck briefing will not suffice to transition the workforce, but instead requires leveraging new network-based social structures and digital tools to broadly increase the uptake of new skills and embed new practice into organizational culture.—Communities for Change, Catherine Shinners

Having said that, change management is above anything else about people—no matter if they are developing or implementing new digital products or going through organizational restructuring, for example—and the WRS focuses on their experience whatever the context.

When I looked at three common change management models—Kotter's 8-Step Change Model, Lewin's Unfreeze, Change, Refreeze, and ADKAR—I noticed that the WRS process can be used as a practice within these frameworks to use community building as a way to attend to the needs of the individuals going through the change.

Let's take Kotter's 8-Step Change Model. Step 2 of this model is to create a "change coalition," a group of people whose role is to work as a team to spread the critical importance of the proposed change and to build momentum around it. At this stage, building a community of practice among this group using the WRS process, will deepen and strengthen the bounds between them, normalize the resistance they will likely be experiencing from other people in the organization, and support coordinated action and influence.

A shared element across all models is the relevance of helping people notice the short-term wins and the progress the individuals and the organization are making toward the change vision. In short, the importance of celebrating small victories. A meaningful way to do this is to invite each person to reflect on what they are learning and achieving on a regular basis—this is where the WRS process can help.

Another critical factor is the identification and elimination of potential knowledge and mindset gaps, and mismatched behaviors and mindsets. The WRS process, as it is based on Experiential Learning Theory, can have a critical role in supporting this necessary learning process.

Lastly, the most important one in my view is the importance of considering, identifying, normalizing, and processing the emotions that will very likely arise during a change process no matter the type: resistance, anger, anxiety, fear, loneliness, inadequacy, disconnection, and shame.

> The experience of going through change at work can mimic that of people who are suffering from grief over the loss of a loved one.—Kandi Wiens and Darin Rowell, Harvard Business Review

The WRS will help you create a safe and judgment-free space for individuals to reflect, share their experience, reconnect with their purpose, realize they are not the only ones going through these emotions, and process and reframe them.

> [the WRS process] creates a space for connection with self and others. I've had some of the most amazing conversations with humans in the space that I don't think I would have had otherwise.—Ray Kanani, RnDAO

These are some of the emotions participants have reported feeling after the sessions (Fig. 4).

Pitfalls

The biggest pitfall in the Weekly Reflection Session process is that the adoption of this initiative is heavily influenced by the often invisible and ingrained dominant cultural assumption that action is more important and valuable than reflection.

> The only tension I've found is that creating space for folx to reflect on what they've learned (silently) for 20 minutes and then can opt-in to share learnings is a tough sell when the world tells you to go go go. I often hear comments like "I'd love to attend but I have other commitments" or "I had a

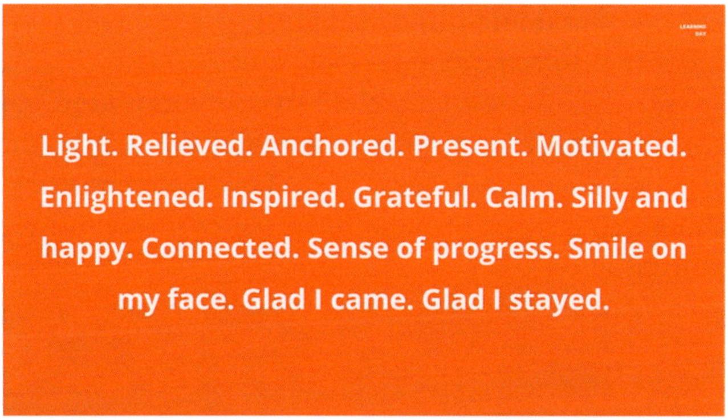

Light. Relieved. Anchored. Present. Motivated. Enlightened. Inspired. Grateful. Calm. Silly and happy. Connected. Sense of progress. Smile on my face. Glad I came. Glad I stayed.

Fig. 4 Examples of how the WRS participants feel at the end of the sessions. Source: Own illustration

really busy week so I couldn't make it." 100% valid and we don't pressure anyone to attend. I do find it interesting though that being busy stops people from slowing down. It's almost like the antidote to your pain is right there but it's so hard to take it.—Ray Kanani, RnDAO

Even if time and other commitments are often used as justifications for not attending the sessions, the truth is that there is a lot of resistance to reflection. Ray from RnDAO and I have experienced this empirically, but others have studied this.

In a study that intended to analyze the tradeoff between doing/practicing more and reflecting/stopping to codify previously accumulated experience when learning a new task, the researchers found that 82% of the participants chose practice over reflection (Di Stefano et al., 2014).

Unsurprisingly for me, they also concluded that this strategy was counterproductive, as the ones who took time to reflect did 23% better in assessment and 19% better in performing the task (Di Stefano et al., 2014).

Even after the participants have decided to join a reflection session, it is essential that they keep joining. This leads us to the next pitfall.

The majority of people who attended the Weekly Reflection Sessions only did it once, even if they gave me extremely positive feedback in terms of the impact this had on their day and week. I assume that joining a session gives folks the gratification of doing something good for themselves, but that doing this consistently, when there is no obligation or concrete metric to achieve, is very difficult.

For the ones who have found the intrinsic motivation to join regularly—some of them seldom missed a session for 2 years!—the benefit is clear. However, I have not yet figured out how to demonstrate this to the people who have not lived through the experience of consistent and systematic reflection.

Practice Tips

The following tips are for the host of the sessions mainly.

What to consider before the session:

- Invite your target group to join an experiment; this makes it less threatening and connects to the mindset of continuous learning.
- Participation should not be mandatory.
- If catering to an international audience and/or coming from different organizations/contexts, offer more than one session time on the same day. At the Learning Community, we started by offering them three times every Thursday, 8:30 AM, 1:30 PM, and 6:15 PM. Recently, we move to Thursday, 8:30 AM, 1:30 PM, in English, and Tuesday at 1:30 PM, in Portuguese.
- Reduce friction: Include an "add to calendar" link in the invitation, and use the video conferencing tool they are used to.
- Adapt the prompt to the change stage or moment the group is in. For example, if it is important to remind the group about how much they have accomplished, you could suggest a prompt like "What am I proud of achieving this week?"
- The prompts should always focus on the personal experience: "what have *I* learned" and not "what have *we* learned."
- Choose your reflection playlist! Music has the power to nudge people into an introspective state—choose it well. You may use our playlist— look for "Weekly Reflection Session" on Spotify.
- Set up automatic reminders to alert the participants to join.
- For more hierarchical organizations, the facilitator should not be the leader. You might bring in someone external, rotate the role or ask for volunteers to host.

What to consider during the session:

- Join the video call a few minutes early and make sure the slides are up and that music is being shared.
- As people start joining the session, stay muted and wave to say hi to them; you do not want to start a conversation at that point nor interrupt the flow of the ones who may have already started their reflections.
- Two minutes before the session transitions from individual reflection to group sharing, the facilitator should send a message on the chat reminding the attendees of what happens next and letting them know that their participation in the second part is optional.
  - Sample message: "We'll move to the second part of this session in 2 min. You can choose to stay or leave.
    In the second part, we're going to share our reflections.
    If you're leaving, thank you for coming!"
- When it is time to move to the second part of the session, make sure to change to the second slide 1 min before stopping the music to give the participants a visual indication, in case they were focused and did not read the message on the chat.
- I have found that most people stay for the second part, but not everyone does. The feedback I have received here was that people were finding the courage to share or that, on that specific week, the reflections felt too personal to share. The facilitator's role, in this case, is to validate that this is OK and that the participant is always welcome to share when they feel ready to.
- The facilitator should read the rules of engagement out loud and remind the participants that they can share as much or as little as they want.
- If the leadership is participating, they should set an example and share their reflections as candidly as they are comfortable too.
- Take anonymized notes of the learnings being shared.
- In the end, ask the group if there is anything else they would like to share before the session closes.

What to consider after the session:

- Collect feedback from the participants; you may choose to send out a feedback survey.
- If relevant, consider adjustments to the format based on the feedback.
- You may choose to send an anonymized recap of the conversation to the group, including the people who were invited to join (see an example below), as a way to support the learning integration and recall, after a few days.
- If relevant, ask the participants to share their experience with others to motivate them to join the next session (Fig. 5).

3   Change Outcome

The desired outcome of the Weekly Reflection Sessions is the process itself, the repetition, and the commitment to learning. The goal is to create a habit, not to achieve a specific state.

From this point of view, I am confident and proud to say that at the Learning Day Community, we are nurturing the habit to reflect on our experiences and turning them into learning. Other community members have shared this and I felt it myself: intentional reflection has become a part of my life, beyond the sessions. I often find myself stopping to observe a certain experience, even if it is for 1 or 5 min before moving on to the next.

Our members have also reported feeling more confident, calmer, in control, connected to their purpose, and more capable of surfing the ebbs and flows of life.

In the case of Municipality Org, it has not been possible to observe if their goals—to support one of their teams to reflect on the meaning and application of their three guiding principles (anti-discrimination, equality, and gender equality)—are being achieved. The person in charge of the initiative left the organization and there still has not been a follow-up.

At RnDAO, Ray Kanani shared the following: "I think we are still very far from what I perceive as a high-functioning learning organism. At RnDAO our mission is to empower humane collaboration. I often ask myself, what are we learning about our mission? What are we doing that is empowering humane collaboration? And what are we doing that is

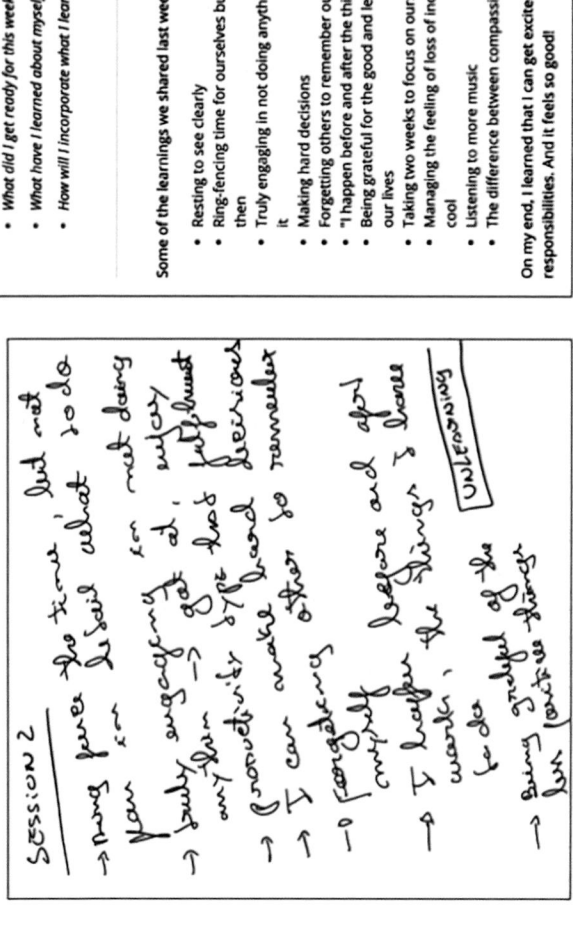

Here are the reflection prompts we used last week:

- *What happened this week?*
- *What did I get ready for this week?*
- *What have I learned about myself, others, and the world?*
- *How will I incorporate what I learned in the rest of the week?*

Some of the learnings we shared last week were about:

- Resting to see clearly
- Ring-fencing time for ourselves but not planning in detail want to do then
- Truly engaging in not doing anything, being good at it and enjoying it
- Making hard decisions
- Forgetting others to remember ourselves
- "I happen before and after the things I have to do"
- Being grateful for the good and less positives things that happen in our lives
- Taking two weeks to focus on ourselves
- Managing the feeling of loss of independence without loosing our cool
- Listening to more music
- The difference between compassion and empathy

On my end, I learned that I can get excited about big projects and responsibilities. And it feels so good!

Fig. 5 A typical screenshot of a recap sent out to the participants after the session

working against our mission? We don't have clarity on these questions, and I think it's because it's easier to do than to learn."

Even if becoming a "high-functioning learning organism" still seems like a distant goal, the input of one of RnDAO's members makes it clear that progress is being made:

> I found the sessions to be very helpful in ways I had not experienced before in a work environment. A deeper understanding of my coworkers as well as an opportunity to become a little vulnerable around issues I am generally sensitive to, such as my health. 5 stars for the process and leadership. Thank you.

4   Final Retrospective

The importance and relevance of individual reflection are unquestionable, both for academics and practitioners. When done collectively, it can help strengthen and deepen the connections that compose any organizational structure.

The Weekly Reflection Session process presents leaders like you with a step-by-step guide to add this powerful tool to your change management toolbox.

If this paper sparked your interest, make an invitation, find a group of people to commit to 45 min a week, keep the consistency, and see the results for yourself. I would love to hear about them. If you would like to experience the process yourself beforehand, you are invited to join the Weekly Reflection Sessions—find more information on our website— https://learningday.community/

References

Di Stefano, G., et al. (2014). Learning by thinking: How reflection aids performance. *SSRN Electronic Journal, 2015*(1). https://doi.org/10.2139/ssrn.2414478

Kolb, D. A. (1984). *Experiential learning: Experience as the source of learning and development*. Prentice Hall.

OECD. (2021). *OECD skills outlook 2021: Learning for life*. OECD. Retrieved October 25, 2022, from https://doi.org/10.1787/0ae365b4-en

Shinners, C. (2016). *Communities for change*. Catherine Shinners' LinkedIn Pulse. Retrieved October 20, 2022, from https://www.linkedin.com/pulse/communities-change-catherine-shinners/

Wiens, K., & Rowell, D. (2018). How to embrace change using emotional intelligence. *Harvard Business Review*. Retrieved January 20, 2023, from https://hbr.org/2018/12/how-to-embrace-change-using-emotional-intelligence

Sara Ramos is passionate about learning and bringing people together to create impactful shared experiences. These passions combined with her restlessness with the status quo, have led her to question what are the alternatives to the way we learn, work, live, and relate to others.

Sara has worked as a facilitator and learning experience designer with clients across different sectors, such as Google (Ireland), Unilever (UK), Invest in Open Infrastructure (USA), Catalyst, and The National Lottery Community Fund COVID-19 Digital Response (UK), the Municipality of Porto (Portugal), Portuguese Women in Tech (Portugal), among many others.

Currently, her focus is on exploring the crossover between lifelong learning and community, as the Founder and Host of the Learning Day Community and the Community Builder at Management 3.0.

Summary and Key Takeaways

Ines Köhler and Cansu Hattula

This chapter summarizes the key lessons learnt based on all contributions of this book. Let us recall the transformation processes that were discussed in the previous chapters. In part one, we looked at the introduction of new digital products and technologies. In part two, we focused on organizational and cultural transformations of digital organizations.

Every Transformation Process Is Unique
One thing becomes very clear when we look at all the transformations discussed throughout this book: every change process is unique. Transformations happen in unique settings. They affect people with different experiences and backgrounds and may trigger individual emotions. Transformations take place in organizations that have their own culture,

I. Köhler
Schindler, Berlin, Germany

C. Hattula (✉)
IU International University of Applied Sciences, Hannover, Germany

leadership style, and systemic dynamics. And of course, the cultural surrounding of a transformation may have an impact on its success as well.

All these systemic and individual factors can influence a change process and its outcome. This is both valid when a company introduces a new technology or a new digital product and valid if we are looking at a cultural or organizational change process. Nevertheless, we spotted some common concepts that are being discussed across different papers and some takeaways that we would like to highlight here.

Think of Change Management and Define Objectives Before the Transformation Is Kicked Off

This is a challenging point as in many transformation processes related to digital products or technologies, there is little time to properly set up an initiative. Often change management is added to the initiative once it has already been kicked off and a timeline has been set.

If there is a way to influence things early on, the definition of realistic objectives is key. Organizations tend to formulate bold, all-encompassing visions at the beginning of a transformation. And they have a purpose—the one to define a "joint dream," a joint ambition. However, it is just as necessary to complement them with down-to-earth, tangible objectives, too. Objectives that can be measured, that give clear orientation for all participants and that may also define what is out of scope.

Clear success criteria and key performance indicators that relate to these objectives not only help to drill down the vision into tangible goals "within reach" for everyone but also give the opportunity to communicate success early on and check in regularly whether the initiative is on track.

Stakeholder Management Is a Vital Piece of Change Management

Stakeholder management is part of almost every change management model. Indeed, it is also mentioned as a learning in many transformation processes described in this book.

The learnings related to stakeholder management discussed mainly relate to these groups:

- The involvement of top management—acting as a sponsor for the transformation.
- The involvement of middle management—acting as a change agent.
- The involvement of the people affected by the change—users in case of software introductions and employees in case of cultural or organizational changes.

"Never start a transformation without the right top management sponsorship!"—everyone has heard this phrase before. And yet it keeps being mentioned in several of the papers. Here it may be necessary to take a closer look at what "top management sponsorship" means. A top management endorsement may help to kick off the change, but for change processes to succeed it is vital that top management makes sure the objectives of all employees working on the transformation are aligned with the desired transformation outcome. Also, an active involvement of top managers in the communication around the transformation and the employee dialogue is key ("walk the talk").

Middle management is the next group to keep in mind when it comes to successful transformations. And this may be particularly challenging. As described in this book—sometimes they are the group most affected by the change. The expectations of their roles may vary throughout a change process. They may lose control, power, or must deal with increased transparency related to their work procedures. Yet their role in the process is key—often employees look up to their managers for guidance. Having a middle management that feels accountable to make the transformation successful and guide their teams through the process is quite critical for a successful outcome. A special challenge occurs—as described—when this group consists of an expert group that may be more reluctant to the change.

As neuroscience tells us, change is related to fear. To counterbalance this effect, it is helpful to have the affected groups involved from the beginning and give them the opportunity to influence the change process. This also matches with the principles of Design Thinking and agile methodologies (e.g., SCRUM). An example would be the full transparency of all documents related to a reorganization. Another one is the frequently discussed use of prototypes or Minimal Viable Products (MVPs) for user testing.

Beware of the Right Change Leadership

There are very different approaches to lead your employees through change. Management by fear is one of them—but the main leadership style discussed in this book is a participative, empathic leadership style or even the vulnerable leadership style described by Würtenberger.

A transparent and compassionate leadership style is the most successful one in achieving sustainable change. The key is to create a feeling of psychological safety and make people feel seen and heard—of course, this is even more challenging if the transformation includes significant changes to the work life of the affected audience. Therefore, transparency also comes with sharing unpleasant outcomes of a change with all affected stakeholders.

Another key element of change leadership is to create space for reflection. This helps to review on emotions related to a change process, on potential solutions and it creates a feeling of community. The article written by Ramos highlights the importance of the reflection process during transformations, for everyone involved.

Your Organizational Culture Affects the Change

The culture of an organization and the right setup play a critical role as well. Several papers mention the positive effect of a so-called "failure culture." During transformations we face a high level of uncertainty. Things are more likely to go wrong than in a controlled environment where we repeat processes already executed a lot of times. Here, an open failure culture helps to see mistakes as part of the process—focus on the learnings and move on. An open failure culture is also key for the actual change management activities. Have the courage to change your approach to change management, your activities, or your setup if it is beneficial for it.

Not always may you have the opportunity to influence the cultural setting your change process takes place in. If you cannot change the organizational culture, it helps to be aware of it and proactively address potential challenges when creating a culture within the team working on the project or the transformation process.

Communication Is Key

The importance of communication is stretched in almost every paper. It is often underestimated although it highly impacts the outcome of a change. Communication comes in on several levels—and starts early in the initiative:

Already during the setup of a project communication helps to translate the defined objectives into a tangible, understandable vision. Creating a compelling story around the objectives and vision is key—the WHY of the transformation—since it is essential to crack the first phases of the ADKAR model: creating awareness for the necessary change and a desire to make the change happen. The story also helps to create a sense of urgency for the employees and ideally a sense of belonging. After the story has been created, it must be told repeatedly, in a language that resonates with the target group.

Keeping all affected stakeholders up to date and informed while the change process is ongoing is the second big communication topic. This is not only about proactive information. It also includes addressing concerns. During the process, a sense of involvement and community is created and there is an opportunity to reflect on the process.

When we talk about communication it is about much more than just sharing information and updates. Creating feedback opportunities and loops is equally important to monitor change outcomes and potential roadblocks. Some papers describe this aptly by giving detailed examples about meeting rituals or surveys.

Another main point related to communication, also discussed by Würtenberger, is the importance of positive language. This is again related to the power of neuroscience and neuro-linguistic-programming (NLP). The language we use impacts our thinking. And the language we use to talk about a transformation process and its outcomes has a tremendous impact on how we may feel about it.

Create a Change Community

Creating a sense of community helps to make change processes more digestible. This is the central topic of the paper written by Ramos. Facilitating a psychologically safe space to reflect on change outcomes, celebrate successes together—all these are aspects of communities and play a big role in the acceptance of a transformation.

Choose Your Change Methodology

As described by D'Aniello, transformation processes often come with new ways of working. This means the transformation process has two elements. The introduction of a new technology and a completely new way of working. This may create twice as much uncertainty and fear within the team.

Here are three takeaways that should be kept in mind. First, make sure the new methodology applied is clearly defined—and not just a buzzword. Second, the team—everyone in the team—involved in the transformation should be aware and trained on the use of the methodology early on. Assuming that "everybody knows what agile is" will not do it. A common understanding, way of working, and language have to be established. And third, make sure the methodology is actually "lived." Some initiatives start as agile but end up in a waterfall scenario.

Summing up all key takeaways, we created a brief checklist for your successful transformation process:

- Take time for the setup phase: define objectives, define a communication strategy, define the resources available for change management.
- Know and involve your stakeholders:
  - Be sure about top management sponsorship.
  - Ensure middle management feels accountable and acts as a change agent.
  - Involve users/employees early on in an interactive way.
- Reflect on your leadership style and lead through the change with compassion and empathy.

- Be aware of the culture your change takes place in—create an open failure culture if possible. Be open to adapt your own approach if necessary.
- Never underestimate the power of good communication.
  - Make sure you have a compelling story.
  - Ensure regular updates about the initiative.
  - Proactively identify and address concerns.
  - Make sure to include feedback loops in your communication.
- If your change process comes with a new methodology, make sure to take sufficient time to introduce it to everyone affected.

We hope that the experiences discussed in the papers, the lessons learnt, the pitfalls shared, and the actionable checklists gave you some inspiration for your next change process.

Ines Köhler is a martech and digital strategy expert with 15 years of industry experience in corporates and start-ups. She has completed her studies of communication science and business administration at Freie Universität of Berlin and LUISS Guido Carli in Rome. Her current role focuses on digital strategy and transformation at Schindler Group. Her previous role at Canto, a leading provider of digital asset management solutions, helped her to get deep insights into the operations of software development and go-to-market strategies for digital products. At Hasso-Plattner Institute she took care of communicating research results and use cases of cutting-edge technologies. Ines is passionate about new work, change management, yoga and personal development.

Cansu Hattula is a professor at IU International University of Applied Sciences and teaches consumer behavior and international marketing to bachelor, master and MBA students. She has completed her studies of business administration at the University of Hannover and her PhD at the University of St. Gallen. Her research interests include change management and marketing strategy. In her PhD, she analyzes how middle management can implement marketing change in their organizations. She gained international working experience in Germany, Switzerland and the UK with various corporations and startups such as Deutsche Messe AG, Too Good To Go and Bayer CropScience. Cansu is passionate about the human side of change management and how to implement new marketing strategies and technologies in organizations.

Zeitfracht Medien GmbH
Ferdinand-Jühlke-Straße 7
99095 Erfurt, Deutschland
produktsicherheit@kolibri360.de